Dream Catcher 48

Stairwell Books //

Dream Catcher 48

Subscriptions to
Dream Catcher
Magazine

£15.00 UK (Two issues inc. p&p)
£22.00 Europe
£25.00 USA and Canada

Cheques should be made
payable to **Dream Catcher**
and sent to:

Dream Catcher Subscriptions
161 Lowther Street
York, YO31 7LZ
UK

+44 1904 733767

argillott@gmail.com

www.dreamcatchermagazine.co.uk
@literaryartsmag
www.stairwellbooks.co.uk
@stairwellbooks

Dream Catcher Magazine

Dream Catcher No. 48

ISSN: 1466-9455

Published by

ISBN: 978-1-913432-88-1

p7

**York UNESCO
City of Media Arts**

Contents – Authors

FEATURED ARTIST
ARTIST STATEMENT: RICHARD MOULTON

"Art is not a mirror held up to reality, but a hammer with which to shape it." As topical kick-offs go, this from German poet and playwright Bertolt Brecht is perhaps a timely reminder of the part played by Art in shattered times. It's tempting to allow disillusionment to dominate the day, especially when the headlines shriek of growing horrors with increasing volume. What, one might ask, can Art do apart from decorate a wall or fill the page of a poetry magazine, especially when innocents are being slaughtered every single day? Such despair does not help. A fragmented world does not benefit from less sensitivity, empathy, or kindness.

It's just as tempting to pick up Brecht's aphorism and get hammering, but that too may lead us down a dangerous road. Art and hammers are not necessarily pleasant bedfellows. To quote another poet and playwright, Oscar Wilde, in the preface to *The Picture of Dorian Gray*, states "All art is quite useless." The master of irony is not this time being ironic. With characteristic epicureanism, Wilde urges us to celebrate the uselessness of true Art. True Art should exist purely to be viewed and appreciated; to be considered; to stimulate thought and discussion. Beyond that, it does not need a purpose. It should not have a use. It should be use-less.

York artist Richard Moulton's collection found herein similarly resist the temptation to paint a world where wrongs are righted and the future is didactically delineated. To be sure, there are scenes of harrowing horror and bristling, coiled violence, unblinkingly considered, and imparted for us to view and be alive to. But its the purpose that imbues them with heft, not the use. Like all great artists, Moulton strives to harness a vision of the world in an inimitable, unique style. His depictions of danger bristle with the clean lines and saturated colours of comic books, with anatomy and movement expertly skewered. His illustrative art opens up a paradigm where it's the purpose, not the propaganda, that encourages us both individually and in groups, to express emotions, commemorate history, expose injustices, overcome obstacles, and gain an understanding of the world around us. In this, Richard Moulton accords with Oscar Wilde, with both diverging from Brecht's sloganeering. Art is not 'a mirror', nor is it 'a hammer' – it exists for its own sake, eschewing function, and, in the hands of painters such as Moulton, wrigglingly alive to inculcate in all of us sensitivity and emotions.

Greg McGee

P<small>AGES OF</small> A<small>RTWORK</small>

There's nothing like the creative process of sequencing an issue of Dream Catcher to send me down all sorts of rabbit holes – and, a bit like any burrowing animal, I emerge after an hour or so in a completely different part of the warren from where I entered. I start with a cup of coffee, take it into the garden where I get snagged on bindweed, and sniffed at by dogs; I wait for my lover to discover how beautiful the constellations of my moles are; decide to have a game of scrabble, and then get distracted by a fresh pack of cards; I bump into priests, dolphins, students; dodge floods and bees, and come back out again, and wonder why it has gone dark (it's an afternoon in late November, dufus).

Then there's the perennial question of What It all Means and How It Should Happen. With prose it seems relatively straightforward. With poetry – who knows? Should it start from emotions, ideas, experiences, or the words themselves? It's no use trying to find a consensus from poets themselves, as we/they all have/had different ideas. Regardless of the juxtaposition I end up creating from your contributions, you are, of course, as readers free to pick your own route through the melée. And whether or not you feel a poem should have responsibilities (as if is lining up to be ticked off in some attendance register of civic duties), I'm sure that it's fruitful to follow Dylan Thomas's assertion in his Poetry Manifesto that 'the best craftsmanship always leaves holes and gaps in the works of the poem so that something that is not in the poem can creep, crawl, flash or thunder in.'

For weeks now, one line from an Auden poem has been clinging on to me – 'we must love one another or die.' It's from his poem 'September 1, 1939,' written on the brink of a global war which is now in the living memory of only a few people. Sadly today's wars are all the more present because of mass media – and will echo in our memories long after they cease. Excavating the Auden poem I was fascinated to learn that he *hated* this line, felt really ashamed of the poem which he felt was too glib, too facile. He suppressed it as much as possible, and when he did allow it to be published he amended it to 'we must love one another and die.' Earlier in the poem are lines which speak to me, today, about what we as writers can do in the face of atrocity, to remember that:

'All I have is a voice
To undo the folded lie.'

And that took me to Pablo Neruda: 'Poetry is an act of peace. Peace goes into the making of a poet as flour goes into the making of bread.'

Poets, story tellers – please keep making bread. And send your loaves to us for inclusion in Dream Catcher.

Hannah Stone

You see the Milky Way in your coffee
and start seeing spirals everywhere:
the old chestnut tree in front of the house,
your boss's eyes, armchair handles,
and the back of your computer mouse.

Late at night, cauled in the laptop's glow,
you're almost hypnotised and swear
the screen's hypnotic glare is dragging
you in like a scene out of *Poltergeist*.
On the other side, you'd find not spirals,

but the B-side to your life: every decision
you never chose, each a tributary
to a river you can never cross. And it goes
down, down, down. What of its end?
There is no plughole — only your head
spinning with regret, and your hands

trying to grip the earth slipping
from your fingers as you look back
to that spot where it all began,
and is now dissolved like the Milky Way
in your coffee.

Christian Ward

LIFE LINE

After coffee in a Keep Calm mug, we explore the salty
basin of my palm – its headwaters, the silted creeks.

Your index finger steers along my life-crease,
glides me towards uncharted days.

When I splay my fingers, an M blushes in the centre
of my palm. M is for mouth, for must, for maybe?

We hold our breath, while Mars conjoins with Venus,
invokes a night seeded with possibility.

The future's in our hands, you say, and close the space
between us until your touch excites

the fine hairs on my neck, and we peel prophecy
from our backs in long, delicious strips.

Claire Booker

LOVELY

my skin, the atlas of my history:
peel back my layers with paint stripper,
fingertips dancing over foreign lands;
the dimples, the creases, the wrinkles increasing,
the fine, fair hairs, the follicles, the flakes;
the ink I chose, the scars that chose me,
each a rediscovery

a constellation of chicken pox across my face;
cat-scratch comet in the soft flesh between forefinger and thumb;
the red dent of an ice-cracked knee,
ready to vocalise displeasure to every staircase;
the blur of a freckle on the vulnerable part of my wrist and
below it, a half-remembered tracery of an older scar;
that tender line – I forget which eye –
on my lid from where in a handful of toddling steps
my infant self learned that things like roses have thorns

and everywhere: stretch marks, tidal impressions of depression
a network charting my passage through time and space

chance and circumstance pictured on my skin,
cratered like the surface of the moon,
but not desolate:
for no one ever looks at the moon and thinks
she is not lovely

Lauren K. Nixon

YOU, SUNLIT

Jeans hang softly from your hips
still unzipped, but knowing their position
instinctively, waistband not yet lipping
your skin. Your arms spread to unveil the morning,
a tongue of light laps your limits, traces your flesh
the way I long to. Day is nipping at our heels,
urging us apart. Threading your belt, you turn,
gilded by subdued rays. At day's end
I will be waiting to be unclipped.

Ali Pardoe

Your heart is a lock.
Give out keys judiciously.
Retain a locksmith.

Reza Ghahremanzadeh

COFFEE SHOP ENCOUNTER

your gaze
pierced me straight through
not the face
I show to the world
but my soul
the real me
known only to myself
I felt naked
vulnerable
but also
entirely liberated

please keep looking at me.

Jagoda Olender

PASS

I'll pass I think, though thank you for asking,
after all it's a good story and I'm flattered to be here,
though not for the asking, but I'll have some
of that wine if you're thinking of passing –

but don't now pass me by for half of me loved
the fluttery flirting, the moment of crisis, the
catching of something irrelevant for a life of
comfort of taking for granted, and inside

I'm laughing. I'll pass you the salt and the words
and I'll pass you my glance for you've spotted there's
someone inside who's a little bit flirty and flighty
like a hat cocked at an angle all covered in netting,

a long-sleeved glove with diamond on the outside,
a finger-tip grasping the tip of each glove end –
but it's much more fun to pass the ball back so the
fun remains just below the eyelids while whispers

are bitching and ladies are raising their eyebrows
in corners of salons, intrigued not by the flighty and flirty
but the actual and sordid – let's stay with the poppy
eyebrows and the hunt for a perfume that passes as exotic,

let's leave the erotic as half-suggested nonsense ...
the tension is better, the novella is better,
the moment is frozen and I never will regret
the making of passes but thank you no,

I'll pass –

but it won't stop me gazing…

Belinda Cooke

EVEN A TREE

I travel along through the beautiful days of the life that I live
marked, as I am, by loves that I found and those that I lost.
Days of good fortune, of caring more tender than lovers should give,
years full of music, happy, effusive, wherever I passed.

How short the adventure, inviting, exciting – the journey I'm on.
And why must I go when I only want more and I'm having such fun?
This lingering kiss, oh! hard as it is, uncertain or, worse,
will come to an end and shadows descend, unfeeling, perverse.

Time is a tango, a frenzied fandango in crimsons and blues.
We take it for granted, until, disenchanted, we falter and lose.
Our memories go, we forget what we know, and – beyond or above –
we finish the story of transient glory; I die for your love.

Ah! even a tree that lives longer than me, must wither and burn
and, turning to embers that no one remembers, can never return.

translated by Philip Dunkerley

PALITO DE MADERA

Caminare despacio por los hermosos días que me toco vivir,
que llenos de arañazos que dejan los amores que sin querer perdí;
colmaron de ventura, cariño y más ternura de la que pueda uno pedir,
los años tan dichosos de música y antojos; allá por donde fui.

Que corto este viaje, que rabia y que coraje, que ganas de seguir.
Porque habré de marcharme, queriendo pues quedarme, quisiera repetir.
Que lánguido este beso tan duro como un hueso, incierto y tan hostil.
Será que hay que dar paso, no hay vida sin ocaso, nostálgico y febril.

El tiempo es como un tango, frenético y fandango, celeste y carmesí.
Se vive acostumbrado, mas luego despojado se muere porque si.
Se pierde la memoria, no queda ni la gloria, si acaso algún rumor.
Que insólito fracaso, sentir que ya de paso, me muero por tu amor.

Qué pena de arbolito, que verde y tan bonito, tenerse que partir.
Palito de madera, ceniza de una hoguera que se ha de consumir.

Javier Bergia

HARDNESS

I love it when we argue.
It makes you feel more real
the way an object feels when you touch it
and your hand doesn't go straight through.
I can feel your edges, the places you won't give.

The night I was locked out, I felt your hardness
in the concrete which carries sound
upwards into bleak sky. I chose a voice
only you would hear, threw dirt at your window
double-glazed, four stories high.

A curtain blinked. When you let me in you asked
how I found you. I counted the stairwells, I say
triangulated the view, retraced steps down corridors
listened for the echo. I scaled your face in my mind
worked out where your eyes should be.

Robin Vaughan-Williams

HE SAT ACROSS FROM HER

once in August in a *trattoria* when the sun set late
when her mind had already rejected him again.

He had a girlfriend, together they were choosing furniture.
She had just been delivered by train from another lover.

He picked her up and she tried to cry on the cliché
of his shoulder scrupulously avoiding his face

as his nose, mouth and tongue always intruded.
The consolation came from his compliments

Your legs have never looked so tanned
she had lain on the beach specifically for this

and now she was faintly pleased. He could please
her sometimes, if she let him. But the thought of his

prominent nose being passed on to their offspring
stopped her. All this wonder would surely start to grate

and she would seek others to betray him. There would
never be an evening when she felt more loved, more loving.

Natalie Fry

The Water Garden

the surface disappears and i am suspended in the deep blue. ▮▮▮▮▮ *i*
glance ▮▮▮▮▮▮▮ *cave* ▮▮▮▮ *omitting azure light. i reach*
out and i think i can almost touch…
▮▮▮▮▮▮*. i remember, now, that we*
▮▮ *must eventually return to the surface…*

to the eternal fountains of rome.

humans create spatial maps everywhere we go.
but somehow this seems to elude me.
every day i am trying to find something in a city i don't know.

when we met here, you said –
i think, you said
i think the rain is a natural mode of existence in this city.

it's haphazard. the walls carved out in layers of bright stone.
each building a new city unfurling out from the old century.
each empire slowly unravelling to be replaced by new worlds each day.

somewhere, here, a new country is arriving…

that summer there was no girl left in me.
so i cracked the wings of twenty butterflies, smearing my eyelids with
neoprene blues.
and i know you thought i was crazier than you.

the rain in trastevere is always a sound at first.

small specks of black ash fall so slow all around us
and i remember, i thought, i must be dreaming, or that we must be the
only people experiencing this exact moment, at the exact same time.
i reach out to try grasp something we can hold here, together
before the world slips through our open hands like water

i open my hand for a moment
and smudge a faint black mark there
the debris of history rushes down before me.
dream.

flocks of a million starlings gather each day in rome
as though it were some strange natural phenomena caused by unseen forces
though we cannot see or explain why this occurs
i search for the reason continuously

Jessica Lim

DREAM POEM

I forgot about your shovel until I did some digging
and found it with your secret, buried in the loam,
like the afternoon you showed your art class how,
exactly, one can draw moths that look like tigers
on a deviant day where the pages are simply not
rubbed white of their plotted guiding lines, and only
an icing sky tops the dainty drawings' steady grey
against the impressionable white of the page.
It was just like that afternoon.

And then there was the dream of arid earth, hands
blackened with soil, and the recovery of the artifacts
either conjured in the mind by chance, or
something you'd lived through before …
Your students are always crying in your dreams.
And it's always your hands pressing on their shoulders
so they can dig their feet into the ground and realise
their secret, which is also your secret: they can live
without what they love, though they shouldn't have to.

Alix Willard

When I have collected the debris,
the casualties from summer's treachery
and winter's rout,
When I have put away the saws
and axes and curse words, sharpened
for a later date,
when I have picked up errant branches,
the final game of spillikins, and cast them
on the fire,
there is still the thin and fragrant litter,
old leaves, twigs and dust
that will stay and haunt me for years.

It was the funeral of an old friend.
I turned up a bleached bone, buried by a long-gone dog.
It was some sort of memorial hidden
amongst the tired and dried out roots.
Too old to be fragrant. It will join the strew,
the scattering of twigs and drying leaves,
as memento that this once was paradise.

Edward Alport

BURIAL RITES

I'll bury these lines where they belong beyond footnote beyond reference
beyond attribution | I buried bones in the garden I buried the garden in my
bones | the garden in my bones grew a skeleton tree twig toes root fingers
feet held high head in earth | I'll bury these lines shift enter shift enter shift
enter send them beyond footnote beyond index frogs at the bottom of a
well they croak and call | these are the nights that we wake in the dark to
scrawl our stories over the bones | I buried the bones in the garden | I grew
a garden in my bones | when I'd lived a day longer than my father | I burnt
my bones down to white powder.

Marius Grose

Narrative # 1

WRITTEN ON SOIL

Scent of wet earth the spade slices down
turns up a head eyes caked with soil
blind years since maybe a child lost its doll
dirt washed from the porcelain head

ghosts of other gardens jostle broken fragments
clay pipes soil filled medicine bottles they surface
through one hundred years of dirt stones roots
spade clunks against something solid with a suck
sound soil releases slate corbel from a fire surround

this patch of land a palimpsest each gardener
overwriting rearranging shaping the soil
but never owning it.

Marius Grose

MEADOW RINGS
After John Clare

This September travellers arrived
with pickups and grey caravans
arranged near the bowling club's tap.

I saw a lad with a bleached quiff
clamber the swings, kick at
the caterpillar climbing frame,
wandering at play in school time.

Police cars were suddenly visible
in Coltsfoot Drive and Celandine.

We witnessed the rec furrowed
with donut circuits and bike tracks.
We locked our doors.

It took the council a fortnight
to evict them: a rickety van
and a green estate abandoned –
doors like wings shaking off rain.

Last week tree trunks appeared
like storm-blown oaks of '87,
nailed in place with steel spikes.

A blackbird, out of sight,
in the highest limb of a tree,
or on a roof ridge – his song
ringing the boundary of his acre.

Sue Spiers

THINKING OF 'LITTLE BOXES' BY MALVINA REYNOLDS WHEN ATTENDING
ANOTHER THERAPY SESSION FOR MY SON

We used to sing a song
at school,
about little boxes
made of ticky tacky.

I didn't know what ticky tacky is,
I used to wonder if it was like Blu Tac,
or masking tape, perhaps PVA glue,

any sticky thing.

Now I know it doesn't matter,
the substance,
just that people try and stick us
into these boxes,

everywhere we turn.

Elisabeth Kelly

FLOATING

If I live in some else's heartland
you don't care, I'm not worth the energy or effort.
The tilted swingometer decides my fate.
The focus groups, my postcode
foretell a simple waste of time.
If you think I'm undecided
and live somewhere especially unsafe
you'll stalk me, send me letters,
knock on my door,
make a megaphone fool of yourself,
promise me the world.
You'll bring your friends tomorrow,
shake my hand, kiss my babies,
kick my daughter's football,
greet me at the village hall door.
I've seen you before;
you're only after one thing.
Once you've got my pencilled kiss
you'll leave me forgotten

never call again

Steve Harrison

THE USUAL
SUSPECTS, A
COUPLING
(from Priti
Patel's
statement to
Parliament,
April/June
2022)

I will make a statement
the children will translate,

control our borders ... by removing the demand
simple demands to be moved to safety.

We cannot sustain ...
cannot sustain.

Our capacity to help ... may be relocated to Rwanda
having no more capacity,

who is considered will be screened and interviewed –
will consider suicide,

our new plan ... it will deter ... make it easier to remove.
every question is a noose

controlling immigration,
faces, names, talents, histories

both legal and illegal
asylum seekers, migrants, refugees.

Last night, we aimed to relocate the first people
by state-backed trafficking.

However... the European Court of Human Rights,
rejected by the Right,

want to make something absolutely clear,
blinded by the light,

anyone released will be tagged while we progress
migration as a crime.

We cannot accept this ... It makes us less safe as a nation.
In a safe life it is hard to imagine

the usual suspects campaign against ... the will of the British.
People setting out on suspicious seas,

the inevitable, last-minute challenges,
ask, as if in their last minutes

systems ... they are firm ... they are fair
will you then, without a heart, consign us?

Sue Johns

MINERS LEANING FORWARDS
after the miners' strike 1984–85

Mortal. Men cropped and cast
into grey corners.

Men as sticks, men as shadow.

Men's pockets lined with bits of string.
Seams. Grit.

Men of rank bound to serve
King Tut and Lord Cardigan.

They gather around hardship money
like new fathers.

Sarah Wimbush

IN THE COMMUNITY

You're in the way, look undecided
lost perhaps, or maybe you've forgotten
where you are or why you've come
or even how to move.

You're in the way. If only you would stand
aside – a foot would do it – you could
take whatever time you need
to orient yourself.

Your move is indecisive
just a shuffling turn, a quarter maybe,
eyes bewildered, slow
like some great ship.

And still you're in the way
you're blocking up the door.
We're edging round you, squeezing past
but no one asks.

Stuart Handysides

A police car parked by the playground,
a young policewoman
with red hair out of a bottle
gives me a friendly smile.

I overhear an old couple: 'That's it.
A homeless person died on the bench.'
I tell it to a tall man who says
I should tell the woman with two dogs.

I'm an unreliable narrator,
when she says lots of shouting
between one and two in the morning,
it leaches into my story.

I walk back past the car.
The window is rolled up.
A blue and white *Do-not-cross* tape
now seals the playground.

I tell a woman with an NHS tag.
'White tent. Gotta be a death,' she says
with a sob in her throat.
'Didn't even have a name.'

At six o'clock they've struck camp,
marquee's been taken down,
a mother and two kids are sitting on the bench
the same maroon as the policewoman's hair.

A mower scatters grass clippings like ash.

Michael Henry

It was late at night as I drove through south Florida, looking for a place to stop for a few hours' sleep. My destination was Key Largo. From there, I would head on to Key West to see Hemingway's home. This was the final leg of one of my cross-country trips. My play had closed in New York, and I was headed home, but taking the long route. I had come down the coast from Kitty Hawk, where I had viewed the Wright Brothers' Memorial. The next few days would bring me across the southern coast to New Orleans, then home. But tonight, I was just looking for a place to sleep.

I spotted a dive motel with fake palm trees and a small courtyard. The office lights were on, as well as the "vacancy" sign. I checked in and got my key.

The courtyard had a couple of wrought iron tables and a scattering of metal chairs, all painted green. Although it was two o'clock in the morning, there were a couple of guys sitting at one of the tables. They had beer bottles and coffee, and apparently nowhere to go. They asked if I'd like to join them for a drink. I pulled up one of the chairs and sat down.

Larry was wiry and dark, and had a fierce intensity about him. Tom was lanky and blond, with a relaxed, easy attitude.

"We' professional dog track gamblers," Tom said, his chin resting on his chest, a proud smile on his face.

"That's right," Larry insisted. "We're professionals." He went to their motel room and brought me a pile of dog track programs as evidence. "See?" he said. "We go to the track every day."

Three years earlier, they had been living in Illinois. Larry had shown up at Tom's apartment, angry and bitter over his girlfriend leaving him. "Let's get out of Illinois," he said. "Let's go somewhere." Tom had suggested either California or Florida. Larry had chosen the latter because it had dog tracks. They had packed up Larry's car and driven non-stop from Illinois to Florida, taking turns driving while the other slept in the back seat.

They had rented a room in this dive motel and headed for the dog track. Quickly broke, they had sold Larry's car and returned to the track to recoup their losses. When that money was gone, they had gotten jobs sweeping out a local restaurant.

"But that's just for money," said Tom. "We' professional dog track gamblers." The words carried the same pride as the first time he had said it.

The motel was run by an old Cuban woman. She came out at one point and asked if they were bothering me. She was smiling when she said it. She hugged Tom around the neck. "These are my boys," she said. "I feed them when they got no food."

They both beamed; she went back into the office.

Together, they made a great story teller. Larry would weave complex tales of the things they had done; Tom would sit silently, then interject some philosophical insight, tying together the things Larry had been saying.

At one point, a hard looking woman with short, dirty hair came into the courtyard and sat down at the table with us. She was taking a break. She was a hooker, they explained; although that's not the word they used. She didn't seem to care one way or another. After a while, she went back to work.

"Why you in Florida?" Tom asked.

I told them I had had a play produced in New York and was now taking a meandering road trip home. Tom was pretty sure he had heard of me. I told him it was unlikely. No, no, he was pretty sure.

A car pulled up. A man in a business suit got out and headed into the office. A few minutes later he came out and started up the stairs. "Do you know what time checkout is?" he said.

"You can check out anytime you like," Tom answered.

The man smiled and nodded.

"But you can never leave," Larry added ominously.

The smile froze on the man's face. He edged up the stairs sideways, never taking his eyes off us. I don't know whether or not he recognized the lines from the Eagles' *Hotel California*, but I don't think he rested easily with the three of us sitting outside his room.

"You should write about us," Tom said.

"I will," I promised. "Someday I'll write a short story about the two of you."

"What will you call it?"

"'Going to the Dogs,'" I said.

"That's us!" shouted Larry.

"That's perfect!" Tom agreed. "Going to the dogs! That's us to a T!"

I had been concerned they might take offense at my play of phrase, but they had obviously reached that place George Orwell had referred to as "the deep underbelly, where you're safe and warm; when you've sunk beneath responsibility, care, or insult."

Larry tore the corner off one of the dog track programs and wrote down their names and his mother's address in Illinois so I could send them royalties someday.

"No," Tom insisted. "He doesn't have to pay us. We' professional dog track gamblers. I just want to see our names written."

I told them I needed to head on to bed. I had a long drive ahead of me.

"You should stay over a day," Larry said. "Go to the dog track with us tomorrow."

It was tempting. I almost stayed over. But I've read Faust, and I've seen the Twilight Zone. I knew I only had one chance to escape being a professional dog track gambler. If I didn't leave by morning, years later you'd have been able to drive into that dive motel and find the three of us, sitting around a table, telling of the night I had arrived, and our adventures at the track, and how I had sold my car to recoup our losses. And how we were all three professional dog track gamblers.

I packed up the next morning and drove on to Key Largo.

But as I sat on the deck of an outdoor seafood restaurant, watching the sunset over the ocean and listening to a mariachi band, I thought of Larry and Tom, and all the characters in all the backwaters around the world. And I lifted my glass in silent tribute to the fascinating, intricate tapestry of life.

Mark Pearce

She always sits in the same window seat,
has the same breakfast: egg and bacon bap.
But today, she smiles as she sips her tea,
reads the paper, leaves a generous tip.
At the till, Joe asks me "You heard who's dead?"
pours my cappuccino foam, mouths the name.
I'm shocked, but not sad. Him, glued to her side,
like a glum shadow she couldn't evade.
Him, counting every coin twice, begrudging
the cost of each item on the chalked list.
"She's taking it well!" we all said, thinking
he was a sour sod who wouldn't be missed.

She brought her new dog next time she came in.
"He was asthmatic," she said with a grin.

J Burke

The storm had brought Eddie. She had said that at the time, his wife, and he thought she genuinely believed it. She had found the dog on the doorstep, when opening the door after breakfast in the morning. It was barely more than a puppy, huddled into a ball, the same white-grey as hailstones, looking up with curious blue eyes circled with grey.

The previous night they had lain awake into the small hours, storm winds whining round the brickwork, rain and sleet hammering on windows. Lightning cracked the sky and she had counted until the thunder came. He let that happen twice before pointing out he had to be up for work in four hours. She raised her head in the darkness, he felt her look at him, but although for years they had counted together from lightning to thunderclap, his mind was focussed on his job. He told her, on the cusp of old age it was time to leave behind childish habits.

In the morning, the costs could be counted: a fence panel askew in the corner of the garden, a neighbour's shed roof blown off, her silence over breakfast. Down the road, a fallen sycamore blocked the street for a day and a half until the council workers came to cut it up. He had had to work from home, although she could get out to her carer's role as it was only a walk away. She took the puppy with her, to look for its owners.

He presumed the puppy must have got loose from someone's garden, been frightened by the noise of the storm and run away. He put a message on the local website and in the post office window. After two weeks no one had come forward and his wife took the notices down, already then besotted by the dog.

She called it after the storm itself, which the Met Office had named Edward. He thought it a poor choice for the dog, a name of ill-luck, ill-fated, although he did not believe in any of that stuff, rooted as he was in his job as a data analyst. He kept his misgivings to himself, although afterwards he regretted not saying something. At least he indicated he did not want a pet, let alone a puppy, all that training and cuddling, the socialising it needed, let alone the way it would tie her down, the way it needed daily walks, the payment of exorbitant vet bills. But the dog stayed, despite what he said.

His wife insisted Eddie was company for her when he was away. He could not deny his job took him away at least once a month for a couple of nights up in London. Before long he realised that, on those nights, his wife would spread a throw over his side of the bed and invite the dog up, although at other times he strictly forbade this. He half believed that the dog came to recognise the sounds as he took the wheeled case down from the cupboard, the motions of packing. It would sit by the bed and watch him with a self-satisfied look in those odd blue-grey eyes.

He made a point of never bringing the dog a present home. To make the point clearer he stopped bringing his wife little gifts as well. He used to pick flowers up at the station, or browse the railway station shops, but after twenty nine years of marriage there was no need for these trifles anymore, in any case. After three decades a couple became solid, indivisible.

Nevertheless, there was no denying the positive effect the dog had had on his wife. She had developed over the years since their son left home, into a lethargic woman, prone to curling up on the sofa and putting on weight. He would not say it to her face, of course, but she had become a pudding of a woman, as his father would have said. He remembered how his father used to call his mother a great pudding, a stuffed sack, a fat cow and how his mother would shout back, the yelling going on over his head, back and forth. He had promised himself he would never behave in that way, so he kept his mouth shut now. Long ago he stopped eating sweets and cakes with her, finished his meals with fastidious precision, never indicating a desire for seconds. He hoped to role model healthy eating, hoped she would follow him in joining a gym. He kept his chocolate consumption to the office where his top desk drawer always had packets of biscuits, boxes of sweet truffles. Despite his efforts, she had got larger and more sedentary.

Eddie took his wife on walks, at least twice a day. She gradually lost weight, slipping back into jeans she had kept for years in the back of the wardrobe against the never-never time she would be thinner. She met other people too, other dog-walkers and started doing longer walks with a group of them. She tried to get him to come along, but he preferred his exercise in the gym, clean, dry, and where he could measure calories burnt, weights lifted, wear shoes that had never touched the ground outside.

When their son visited, he admired his mother's activity and let the dog up onto his lap. He had always shared his mother's tendency for superstition, bright clothes, a belief in luck or karma. Before long, their son and his husband had got themselves a dog too and suddenly they were off on weekends with their mother/mother-in-law to walk along beaches where dogs were welcome, to start a year-long project of walking the Pennine Way, one weekend at a time. He was invited, even pressed, to join but refused it all, not liking the smug look Eddie shot him out of the corner of those blue-grey eyes, not liking the dishevelled look of his wife returning from those windswept places when all she could talk about was the long line of the horizon stretched out before her, sunlight and wind against her face.

He liked those weekends to himself, quiet islands between the working weeks. His wife would leave him meals in the freezer. He could watch whatever he liked on the TV.

He noticed his wife was buying new clothes. Even those slim jeans slid off her now. She started wearing dresses, skirts, things she had always said she could not wear before because of the width of her thighs, her cushion of a bottom. Then she had her long hair cut short and one evening, walking up the drive, coming home, he caught sight of a woman with a slender neck and outstretched arms, dress floating round her, dancing in the kitchen, who he did not recognise until the dog barked excitedly and he heard her voice, laughing. Another time, he was sat at the desk in the study, glimpsed a pair of slender legs running up the stairs and was in the hallway checking for intruders, before he realised it was his wife, the dog bounding at her heels.

When she said to him, not long after these moments, that she thought things between them were not working very well, he agreed with her. She suggested perhaps they could try couples' counselling or marriage guidance, but he was taken aback by this, even more so that she had leaflets to hand, a link saved on the laptop. He said then that he thought they were comfortable. She said, "We do not do anything together anymore." He had laughed out loud then. "We live together, we are married," he exclaimed. She had not even smiled at that, said that they did not share any interests, that he did not even like Eddie.

He had looked down then and straight into those blue-grey eyes looking up at him, surrounded by fur the colour of storm clouds, the dog's tongue lolling out, the palest pink, as if the dog were laughing at him.

"No", he said, "I always thought the dog was a mistake."

"I needed something that loved me unconditionally," she said.

"You have me," he responded.

"Yes, that's interesting, don't you think?" she had replied, looking away, over his shoulder.

He had no idea what she meant by that. He suspected counselling would be full of such ambiguous sentences and endless talk in circles. He had refused to go. All couples got through good and bad patches, he thought. Things would be different again in six years' time when he retired, with luck the dog would be gone by then as well. Time enough then to talk in circles if she wanted.

Things retained their usual pattern. He came home each weekday evening to a cooked meal which they ate in front of the TV news at seven. Then his wife would take Eddie out for his final walk, sometimes calling into the local pub for a chat with those dog-walking friends. He would be in bed reading by the time she got back. She would catch up on work emails in the kitchen, often not coming to bed until he was asleep. At weekends while she was off on long walks, he would go to the gym, doze in front of the sport in the afternoon or mow the lawn, if the weather was good enough.

This year the annual work conference was in Bournemouth. It was an irritation, from where he lived, it meant going for an extra night. Three nights away. He could have taken her with him, but, as he said to her, it was not her kind of thing.

She had looked at him for a long moment, said, "Are you sure?"

He said, packing his briefcase for the morning, "Well yes, you would have had to make arrangements for the dog, in any case, which would be an additional expense."

After Bournemouth, when he gets home, she has left.

There is a note on the dining room table – more formal, he feels, than leaving it on the kitchen table. Her handwriting, as familiar as his own, tells him she knows the marriage was over, that she has taken half and been as fair as she could but, of course, she has taken Eddie. She has told their son, but he already knew, she writes, before anything was said he knew. The note sits on a letter from her solicitor, advising him divorce proceedings are being instigated, that mediation is the preferred avenue, that the usual settlement in 'these cases', where children of the family are no longer dependant, is a 50/50 split.

Her wardrobe is empty. Most of the books in the house were hers and bookshelves gape across the rooms like awkward mouths with teeth removed. She has left all the ornaments inherited from his mother, taken all those from her own parents, taken half the family photos, half the pictures off the walls, half the crystal wine glasses, one of the two dinner services. She has taken the Le Creuset casserole but left the saucepans. In their bedroom, her side of the chest of drawers is clear, the jewellery box gone, except her wedding and engagement rings, never before off her fingers, side by side in the dust on his half. For the longest moment he cannot take his eyes away from the rings.

Halfway down the stairs there remains a photo of Eddie, in a glass frame, as a puppy just after he turned up in the storm, staring out at him with those oddly clear blue eyes, chipped out of a long gone summer sky. He takes the picture from the wall, breaks it across his knee where it cracks with a sound like lightning, he finds himself counting for the thunder under his breath and throws the picture down the stairs.

Sarah Hills

LATELY

Someone has taken over my attic.
All day she stays quiet
but for a shuffle and a heartbeat.

At night she slip-slops down the stairs,
scrabbles through drawers, dishevels the wardrobe
and smears all the windows.

She disorders the bookshelves, deranges pictures,
unhinges boxes, muddles photographs
and paints nightmares in the kitchen.

She smudges the television screen,
turns the volume down
and the central heating up.

On the computer she hides Documents,
removes words from Wictionary
and disconnects Wikipedia.

Since she came the house has loose slates.
Walls crack, boards creak, damp seeps.
I fear she's undermining the foundations.

Alice Harrison

She holds a rack of letters in her hand,
Stares quizzically through gold-rimmed bifocals
At them. " Oh damn, I can't go where I'd planned,"
She says, bemoaning a glut of vowels.
"Would you believe I've got three E's, an I,
And very little else? A blank, dear? No,
No blanks." Surveying the board, she casts her eye
In search of somewhere else where she can go.
A study in silent concentration
She sits, hunched and unmoving, in her chair.
At last she stirs, leans forward, one by one,
To finish on a Triple Word Score square
Lays down all seven letters on the board.
"Reindeer!" she chortles, keeper of the word hoard.

George Jowett

NEW SUIT

What card is this that circumstance has played?
Not joker, deuce, a jack an ace or queen,
you're neither heart nor diamond, club nor spade.

It's quite a mad impression that you've made,
unparalleled in depth and unforeseen.
What card is this that circumstance has played?

I'm taken with this crazy cavalcade,
ignoring all conventions, all routine.
You're neither heart nor diamond, club nor spade.

I'll gather up my dog-eared deck to trade
for something new, for something still pristine.
What card is this that circumstance has played?

I'm ninety parts intrigued but ten afraid
of what this novel suit may come to mean.
You're neither heart nor diamond, club nor spade.

Are you the deity to whom I've prayed,
Beelzebub or somewhere in between?
What card is this that circumstance has played?
You're neither heart nor diamond, club nor spade.

Chris Scriven

SUMMER
SOLSTICE

I am pacing in the garden
thinking of what I could say,
and what I really mean
to me; when the estranged
gods become absolved gods,
when I see the black spider
half in, half out the hole
in the wall, encircled
by a shock of web and I love
it, would wear its likeness
on a black string and know
too often do we kill the things
we want to be; when the spider
neither attacks nor retreats
and I know I cannot be cursed
if I can do my work
on the days I don't feel like
being kind and giving
directions to the stranger
who takes a seat next to me
in a room of many free seats;
if I can mind losing
the first few minutes of piano
music on a latest release;
if I can look up at the clouds,
the blown-glass air we can see,
and fall asleep in the sun,
dreaming of being full
of paper instead of water,
and the clasped forearms
sky and sea make, of a tree
and its branches spilling
over a derelict house, still
in half blossom; if the day is long
and the sun is high and hot
and I can look at it long enough
to care.

Alix Willard

SOFT WATER

This glass of Welsh hill water
comes from rain
that sluices through
avenues of Sitka spruce,
that batters misshapen
hawthorns on the moor,

it is of moss, trout
and lost tarmac roads,
of roof slates
from the drowned *hafod*,

has reflections of Ospreys;
bright, rippling,
piercing *Llyn Brenig*,

has filtered through
platform cairn,
charcoal, bones
and ancient grain,

brings the pain of growth,
as shoots burst out
of the comfortable dark,

comes from snow,
apart from the flakes
captured by the girls from *Fron Heulog*
who between sledging rides,
stand open mouthed to the sky –
soft marshmallows of cold
melting on their tongues.

Diana Sanders

small   fenced off   too up and down
for the farmer's plough   timber's profit
just landmark now

one small track   north to south
is all that remains of the tread
of men's feet

the rest long forgotten   a tangle
of wild impassable undergrowth
thorns and roots

i am its guardian   chronicler   bard
shift through its layers of shadows
leave no mark

i am soil made man   gnarled as bark
tendrilled   twisted   voiceless
always here

some nights I drift to its heights   gaze down
over meadows   homesteads   bathed by
clear skies

i haunt the track's edges   merge into trees by
the boundary's barbed gate   look for lights
ascending

but no one comes
no one comes

Patricia Leighton

WE NEED TO TALK ABOUT YOUR BINDWEED PROBLEM

In this Spanish summer garden
your solanum's rampant as a scandent harlot
vaunting and vining up the nearest tine.
I too shimmy these javelins of jasmine
a diocese of dark isosceles
the shape of the bottom jaw of a snake
seen too late, from underneath.
Do you think I don't hear you sigh
when you see me? Lady, you say
I stalk your thoughts. Might I suggest
you're obsessed? You want me dead
but keep a tendril by your bed, pack me
like a locket in your nightgown pocket.
Down here in what you call no-man's-land
did you not expect to have to wrestle with the earth?
I watch you before me, squat then rise,
each time with fistfuls, lungfuls of leaves.
Even as you grip
my thin white root and snip
I'm spinning my vine
up an unseen stem of your mind.
What is it in me that you dread?
All the rooms you've never entered
uninvited, your forever epiphytic friends?
It amuses me to have you here
on your knees, wanting to talk
what constitutes consent. What is this garden
if not a covenant you've broken?
But in the end, without belief
even Eden twists to Need.
Ten tendrils five fingers
two opposable thumbs.
A necklace of petalled confetti
and – lazily – your boundaries lost.
It's only when I latch the apple sapling
that something in you snags. I watch you gasp,
sink back on your hunkers, clamp your palm
to your Adam's apple. Now you object
to snare over air. Now you
make the connection.

Julie Sheridan

ON NOT BEING A SWINGER OF BIRCHES

Well, I might have become a swinger of birches for a while;
instead, I avoided what I saw as the risk
by not lacking in guile.

Normally, I'd chide off the threats, one against another,
staying clear of the swing of the swingers; hoping
they'd ignore me – too weathered to bother.

But you ask me why – in every circumstance – I am as
I am: gainsaying regret; somewhat crispy;
something of a shivery man?

Together with idealists, I'm familiar with the Judas-tainted night,
plowing (unsuccessfully) through all those
legacies, drenched in spite.

In a kitchen or two I've been hung on the marinating hook,
the one used by hypocrites against do-gooders hoping
to uncouple truth.

I was once an all-weather guide in the Pyrenees of conscience;
I resigned – vertigo with excuses;
couldn't keep my balance.

Later, I side-walked with ruptured minds (wishing for recovery) –
like me, harassed by shoals of steel deceit, victims
of their own peculiar thuggery.

I've escorted flocks of unsold figurines, my Self close to hand,
always yearning for the wise and the noble – looking for
the grandeur of the grand.

Of course, none of this explains why the benediction still eludes me –
sewn-up folds within folds inside a life:
concord without the tea …

Even so, sometimes I wish that I'd been a swinger of birches.
A delusion, of course. Imagine me with the ghosts of confessions –
alone – in derelict churches!

Harry Hendrick

Father Pascal has a puncture, has phoned
to say he's getting a taxi. In the church,
rows of uniformed children slide on shiny pews,
heedless of their teachers' insistent prayer, Shhh.
A child points and delighted giggles
bubble as heads turn to follow a foil balloon
drifting along the aisle. Then a scrap of trembling red
is spied – rising and falling

like notes in a hymn. Even the priest, rushing in,
raising arms draped in red and gold
can't distract furtive eyes from glancing up
to watch the balloon and the butterfly
nudge against the ceiling,
lost souls searching for heaven.

Alex Toms

BEYOND BELIEF
(Reims – Notre Dame 1914)

this creased photo of two priests,
their white hair glinting in sunlight
shining on ruins – lashed remnants
of the chosen cathedral for crowning kings –
roofless now, crashed and battered
by shell bursts, set on fire with raging flames,
melted lead trickling through the gargoyles –
black rosary beads slithering to the ground.

In their long, dust-covered cassocks
they seem lost, vacant – gazing into nowhere,
feet sunk behind fractured stones – fragments
of arches and altars, Canterbury caps gripped
tightly in their left hands – in case they drop.

Marion Ashton

PERSISTENCE

I wandered through the mind of Dalí;
Twisted through canals of madness
Born of fears that we suppress,
Desires that both mislead and guide me.

In the crypt I banished gratefully
The hours and minutes of time's caress –
The illusion of humanity's progress
That keeps us in creative slavery.

Discarding self-made shackles in the sun,
I danced and shivered in the Samhain moon
And let my rational become undone.

My heart now sang a mesmerising tune;
The paranoiac process had begun!
I followed memory in the new aeon.

Jim Sinclair

GIRL BY A WINDOW
After Matisse

Her mind, a suitcase unpacking details
of an argument with her lover, her arms

folded in disdain over white ruffles
stitched to the silkness of her blouse,

she can feel the gold claws grasping
the diamond on her finger catch

there and her body stays motionless
staring out but seeing nothing. Her red lips

bruise her face, her nose bent in thought.
Balmy trees shake in the breeze and do not

burn through the barrier, a glass encasement
she doesn't want to rip apart. The pavements

are clean with spring and hope. Her mind,
midwinter and an accumulation of fog. The noise

and busyness of a riviera promenade, the traffic
that will start when the sun begins to fade.

Natalie Fry

TEACHING ICARUS TO FLY

After seeing him off, I watch
him melt into the morning light
like a lava lamp globule, slowly
becoming one with sky and cloud.

Last week, I helped tame his feathers
with a lamp and trained him
to roll past 747s in the garden.
Convinced he knew more

than the Wright Brothers, a trial run
at Crystal Palace smacked him against
a double decker. Kids laughed
and posted TikTok videos. Drivers

sighed. We pored over Da Vinci's
ornithopter plans in the potting
shed and watched footage of geese
taking flight until our bodies sweated

oil; quacking at one another
in the early hours. At dusk we drove
to the South Downs and practised
take-offs and landings until the earth

was insect-like. When his feet lifted
off for an inch or two, I knew then
he must go. Waking, I heard robins
securing the lawn. Fireflies lit a runaway

ready for me to say goodbye and meet
him in some other place where we might
collide into each other, breathless
from a lifetime's uncertain path.

Christian Ward

FIRST AUTUMN, LEEDS

Sodden leaves everywhere,
dull light glows from a warm café.
Lecturers too abstruse today;
overpriced cheese rolls,
a fusillade of pinball scores,
steaming mgs of tea.

Outside, art students come and go
talking of Goya and Gericault;
long woollen scarves
dangle round their skirts
as the breeze chills them forward
towards the Parkinson.

Home at dusk down narrow streets
headlamp beams through fog.
I'm a newcomer here, my turn
for poetry in shabby rooms
as kids play on waste ground,
gratuitous in puddles.

John Short

SHADOWGRAPH 11
the extended veils
(poetry detected in kai m. siegbahn's nobel physics lecture, 1981)

i

modern –
reasonably
small people! (

the finger prince.)
science in the
hands of the

state

ii

feeling good
in the lab? (*meta-*
physical; 'the finest

meshes of the net.') the
competitive edge of the
world. (table – 'the gi-

ant leaps…') our en-
tropic hero! 'radi-
ant' – *veil fall-*

ing

Sean Howard

iii

'morning after,' man &
mirror… (the bomb's down-
town core.) the mosque turn-

ed into a shoe store. (god sent
through the male?) *at the summit,*
the peak disappears… (jihad? all-

ah splitting his sides!) sex; sighs
matter… *returning the man th-*
rough the slit. (atomic: world

wide?) 'the primitive pho-
to-effect' – *feeling the*
light freeze in my

eyes

iv

the editors
of nature. (*the*
puppets' theatre.) the

playing dead. all it
takes, 'the slight
touch of a fin-

ger'

APRIL POEM # 2

I will just catch that 15 minutes
when the sun is still on the garden
and fills the magnolia flutes
with a creamy light that spills and slips
warming my bones kept
in the old north-facing room

and the pair of blue tits watch me
as I unwind from this day of days
hands wrapped on a mug of tea
thoughts in a dark fjord night
of horror with Jon Fosse

the magnolia is all the light there is
and Fosses dark fires cannot reach
across the ocean and the rooftops
so I will roast some potatoes
and soon she will be home

I will just catch those 15 minutes

Nick Allen

APRIL POEM #4

and the night was dark
there was just enough blue
for the sky not to be black

and the pink of the cups
shone through cream
veins through old hands

making the blossom
seem less than white
less than glowing
more like stretched skin

Nick Allen

Like a string of marshalled ducklings
my son's letters of scientific qualification
allow him to understand the miracle of
photosynthesis, lend an unquestioned
grasp of metamorphosis.

We trail amongst these giant pines,
catch a glimpse of the spilt pink
sunset, remark on the atmospheric
phenomena, how it weeps
across the retina.

*This vision we must preserve
safe in imagination.* Though I know
he snorts at my clinging
to Keats, who knew of blood
and how the bright star heart beats.

The green robed senators around us
carry their own tale,
remember how he charged through here
in infancy, tripped on a root
and pronounced quite fiercely,

not that this is a prop,
a type of aerial growing out from the stem
and down into the ground,
but announced in passionate tones:
this is proof of dinosaur bones.

John Irving Clarke

standing in the ocean that day, I was observing the evening light. it's all
pale pink and purple hues. you turn back and glance a smile at me,
showing off your brand new teeth
just as the light glanced off the crest of a wave, *i remember, now,* how
light will always take the fastest path to the surface.

before it drifts into the small century of the sky...

once, on the dunes at whale bay, you wrapped me up in a wool quilt
and told me the story about the Princess of the Sea –
who, you say, crossed the miles of vexed water, like Te Rau-o-te-Rangi,
without fear of wave or shark
with only daughter upon her back.
it was summer, as it is always summer in this dream.
and when you passed, I wanted to give you to the ocean.

I try not to think of all the things I have lost.

Jessica Lim

Or maybe it happens like this. You're in a queue so long it might stretch further than the moon, but there's no chit-chat, no solidarity, everyone stays silent, staring at their shoes. From time to time a gap opens up & you all shuffle forward. When you reach the front, if you ever reach the front, you'll hold out your hand, await the ink stamp of unacceptability colour-coded according to infringement that not even Coca-Cola will wash off & then some colossus will step forward, seize each of you by the wrists, swing you in five full rotations above its head & let go, sending you flying over ramparts into distant tree-tops where you'll lodge like minor celestial bodies. Not one of you will have anything to shine about.

Deborah Harvey

Narrative # 2

A prolonged pianissimo. Then silence.

Rhythm must have been the easiest to hold on to
as it pulsed through your hands, your body.
But you internalised the whole trinity
of rhythm, melody and harmony;
everything carried forward in your contrapuntal mind
against the pull of silence.

Perhaps long before the silence reached its crescendo,
or just before a final chord, or after bargaining with God,
or just when a dying note tugged at you,
your brain slipped into a new key,
rededicating portions of itself
to soundless composition.

With all the tools drummed up from far and wide –
horns, ear trumpets, resonators arcing your Broadwood –
you set about adapting.
Pounding the piano with little feedback from your ears,
poring over scores, you made your eyes your interpreters,
your pen collide with the paper.

If some find freedom in a prison cell, rosy-fingered dawns
in blindness, passion in paralysis,
if wings are kept in store for caterpillars,
then why should you not have found melody in muteness,
whirlwinds in silence, or the infinite interwovenness
of a Great Fugue.

Judith Wilkinson

Crawford turned off the highway down a red dirt track, which wound between gum trees and the signs of what he might call an indigenous community. A busted-up ute, crashed into a tree trunk and abandoned, the tyres long gone, the paint flaking. An old government sign saying 'Liquor Act, Restricted Area', with assorted whisky and port bottles arranged underneath, glinting in the sun like a sequined miniskirt. He drove slowly past the homesteads. There were lots of dogs and lots of kids. He noticed an outside tap that had been left running, the water making a pool of red mud. A group of people were having an argument on a veranda. There was finger-pointing and rapid swearing, the swear words merging in a flowing way that wasn't quite his English. He supposed government funds had gone into the homes. And there were jobs around here, four or five miles from the airport, where wealthy tourists flew in to take some snaps of Ayers Rock, went goggle-eyed at some dot paintings and then flew out. He knew that it was Uluru now, but it was hard to change what you had learned in childhood.

He followed the Satnav to the padlocked gate that marked the perimeter of the land that had been leased to the ranching company. A chain link fence ran somewhat pointlessly for fifty metres to his left before ending at the dry river bed. He got out and pulled the keys from his pocket, picking through them to find one for the padlock. Orange-billed zebra finches flew past, cheeping, though he didn't notice them. Neither did he notice the elderly man sitting on a rock in the acacia scrub to his right.

"Too dry for stock," said the man. "And your dam's no good. Dam's never no good. No want 'em."

Crawford turned slowly, expression neutral, and straightened up. The man was thin, wiry, and crazy-haired, the skin around his throat loose and dark with a spider's web tracery of many lines. One eye was sealed shut and leaking, like a bruised plum, the other fixed on Crawford in a frank stare.

Crawford nodded. "Is that so? Well, I'm not a stockman myself."

"What ya doin' here then?" Looking over the car. Crawford moved to the padlock.

"Just looking at the land," he said. He was here to survey it for use as a solar farm.

"The land don't speak to you. It talk to us. This mother country, granny country."

"Sure," said Crawford.

"So what ya lookin' for?"

Crawford opened the padlock and swung the gate open.

"Sunshine," he said.

The man snorted, then returned to the long stick that he was carving with a pocket knife.

Crawford drove the car through, then shut the gate behind him. The dirt track snaked between rocky outcrops and scrub, until the land opened out into a plain of thin grass. Just before the plain, the bleached trunk of a dead gum tree lay across the track like a skeletal finger. Fallen or pushed? It didn't matter, it wasn't a huge site. He turned the engine off and took his theodolite from the boot. He slung a small water bottle and a chilled flapjack into his backpack and set off on foot. Before long he had the tripod up and began checking distances and the incline of the ground. That would affect how the panels were set up. Then he needed a quick inspection of the power line, a mile away across the plain. He made sure he could see it with binoculars and set off. As he went he looked at the ground conditions and considered the flow of water, should it rain; a cloudburst could lead to flash floods. But the land here was flat, gently inclined, and it wouldn't be an issue.

The country was empty: red dirt, patchy grass, anthills and scrubby bushes that were mostly thorns. Heat haze, that slippery genie, inhabited the void. If you thought you could see water in the distance, then you were probably in trouble. He stopped to use a GPS measuring tool to check his location. Not far from the centre of the property. GPS was vital out here: physical boundaries didn't exist, or were often in the wrong place. GPS could tell you where people should and shouldn't be.

Despite his broad-brimmed hat he was working up a sweat and his collar was chafing. He swigged some water from his bottle and checked he could still see the power line. When he took off his shades to wipe his face, the glare stung his eyes like gravel. He replaced his shades, took a deep breath and strode forward. He'd get there and back quickly, return to the car and stick the AC on. Before long he was at the power line, making a visual inspection of its condition, checking that the voltage was what they'd been told.

When he turned to go back, he realised that he didn't have an obvious landmark in the distance, only a few gum trees on the horizon and a fold in the land which he suspected marked the position of the road. But he had GPS. His stride was confident, though he felt like an ant in a big, orange-red bowl, searching for something sweet, drawn ineluctably into the middle, the focal point, where the sides of the bowl rose around him in cliffs of hot red rock. Where anyone looking into the bowl would surely squash him. He didn't have agoraphobia. You just forgot how empty the land was out here, you would swear you could see the curvature of the earth. He had to sit and get some water. There was nowhere to sit. He turned about, spotted a rock about thirty yards away and made for it. He sat, drank heavily, found his flapjack. The butter had oozed out and sat in a pool against the cling film. He tossed it, checked his phone. No signal. Well, he'd known that. He removed the GPS tool from his pack. It was still in the mode for the survey, so he switched mode, fumbled and dropped it. There was a rattling noise which suggested a battery had come loose. He'd need a screwdriver to open the back, best to get moving. Not half a mile to the car, for sure.

His strides soon shortened as his leg muscles began to cramp. He thought about putting the theodolite and tripod down, coming back for it later. Crazy talk, he wouldn't find it. He raised his hand to his cheek to brush off a bluebottle, and noticed that his breath was coming in tight little bursts. His ears were flushed, felt like they would burn up, and his ear drums bounced to his heartbeat. It was nearly midday. The sunlight hung on his shoulders as heavy as lead.

Shade was what he needed. He headed for the gum trees in the distance and hoped that his legs didn't give out. His muscle cramps were spiking. Then he started muttering the Lord's Prayer, unexpected, in spite of himself.

He got to the gum trees just as his vision started to wobble. He threw the equipment down, then fell over sideways into the shade, the red sand biting his cheek. He pulled his hat off and lay there, panting like a dog.

Sometime later he heard voices.

"That 'im down there."

"Jesus, Dad. He doesn't look too good. Hey, fella? Hey mister can you hear me? Come and help me sit him up. Yeah, you hold that arm. Christ he's a heavy bastard."

Crawford helped push himself up and looked about him. A young woman squatted in front of him. She wore denim shorts and a festival T-shirt, and was staring at him intently. Her hair was in neat braids, her dark eyes laughed between narrow lids and her lips were compressed in a mix of concern and distaste. Her skin was deep brown and shone like a polished stone.

"Hey fella, can you tell me what day it is?"

Crawford felt overly taxed.

"What's your name?"

"Colin." More of a whisper.

"I'll get a can of water, Colin. You stay with him, Dad. Lucky for you I'm off for the day."

The old man with the diseased eye was leaning against a tree, still carving the stick. It was a walking stick covered in dots and lines, a snake or lizard making its way around the handle. Colin blinked at him.

"She nearly done," said the man. "Varnish her up, get me two hundred bucks."

"Right," said Colin, with surprise. He felt like slumping backwards.

"No, no. You stay sit."

Colin sat. He could sense the disdain in the man's voice.

"You know where find water?"

Colin shook his head.

"You follow the finches." The man chuckled.

A while later the woman returned carrying a large plastic can of water. She unscrewed the cap, and without asking permission emptied half the can over Crawford's head and shoulders. He gasped in shock.

"Now drink some." She lifted the big can to his lips. The water was cold and earthy. "You'll feel better in a few ticks," she said.

A while later Crawford cleared his throat, took a few deep breaths, shifted so his back was against a tree trunk. His heart rate was coming down. A headache was massing like a thundercloud but he welcomed it; he knew it was his body finding its way back.

The woman sat opposite him, arms around her knees. She waited, watching Crawford regain some alertness. Like a hunter, he thought.

"Thank you," said Crawford, a few minutes later.

"So what are you doing here? Dad said you were looking for sunshine." She laughed.

"I'm doing a survey. For a solar farm."

She nodded. "Yeah, we heard about the plans. People don't want it here, really."

"Well cattle ranching hasn't worked out, so…"

"The cattle were here for what, maybe four years. We've been here a lot longer than that."

"You're not doing anything with the land, though are you? I mean productively?" He wasn't in a good place for this conversation, but he didn't feel like trying to find his way back to the car. Not yet. The woman sighed and glanced at her father.

"This land don't like you. It make you bitter inside," said the old man.

"But I'm with the good guys," said Crawford, vexed. "I mean, solar power is clean. We're not burning coal, we're not digging up the land."

The woman's eyes hardened. "Okay. And how much power do you think my mob use? No, this electricity will go to hotels and bars with big AC units so that tourists and people like you can hide from the heat. And our land gets covered in cables and panels."

"I don't decide what happens."

"I bet you could say it should go somewhere else."

Crawford shrugged weakly.

"I've taken water from our waterhole and poured it over your head. D' ya know what that means? It means you're not a stranger any more. You have to listen to me."

"I'm under no obligation!"

"And I probably saved your life."

Crawford looked at the red dirt, the scuzzy little bushes. He didn't talk to these kinds of people unless he had to. They were often drunk or aggressive, and he had nothing but his rightness to fall back on, and stating his rightness never seemed to help much. And here he was in a proper fix. There was an alternative site, he was supposed to be looking at it this afternoon.

"The company that has the lease from the government will make the decision. I expect they'll sell the lease to the solar company," he said. It felt pathetic.

"Not if you tell the solar company it's no good?"

He floundered. "I didn't know there was a waterhole out here."

"'Bout two hundred metres that way."

Off the site, he thought. Just about. If he had his bearings now.

"Not on the leased land, though, is it?" he asked. She tilted her head, cynicism rising. She had looked prettier before.

"The water runs through this land," she said. "Over it, when it rains. We know the paths."

"My fellas hunt here," said the old man. "Good for roo shootin'. This land our land. Our Dreaming. You look here, you see money for someone. Money is the whitefella Dreaming." He jabbed a finger as spoke. Crawford ignored him, looked at the woman, earnestly.

"Can you take me to the waterhole, please? And then, maybe back to my car?"

"Are you good for that?" she asked.

"I think so. I'll leave my kit here and, and come back for it." His doubts screamed that it would disappear, but he wanted to show that he was trusting them.

"Okay."

He trudged slowly through the shade, through gum trees and thick acacia scrub, the shadows of birds flitting between branches. Eventually they reached a curved, sandy depression. At the bottom was a bathtub sized puddle, he couldn't tell how deep.

"We say the river comes up here for air," said the woman. "Without this water – "

Crawford raised a hand and nodded rapidly. Their eyes locked.

"I don't think I asked your name?"

"No, you didn't. It's Mirrin."

"I'm going back to my car, now, Mirrin. But thank you. This has been useful."

She laughed, perhaps in a mocking way, perhaps despairingly, he didn't understand. Looking up, away into the silver-green gum leaves, a laugh that was musical but mirthless.

Half an hour later he was back in the car with the AC on, driving into town. He had wanted to leave the site immediately, but now he pulled over and readied his phone. If he was going to do this, he needed to do it now.

"Michael, how's it going? Yeah, I've taken a look south of the power line, the ranching company land... Not sure it's ideal, there are dry watercourses cris-crossing the site, big waterhole on the edge, it's a definite flash flood risk … Yeah, that's right. I was gonna look this afternoon, but I've got a touch of heatstroke... yeah, I know. Thanks. I'll get on it tomorrow. In any case, I don't think you're gonna want to put it there." A few seconds later, he hung up.

He didn't know if he felt dirty or clean.

Mirrin finished eating the packet rice and flung her teacher ID on its lanyard around her neck, grabbing her car keys out the bowl. Her Dad stood in the doorway.

"Ya going in now?"

"I got a call from Saunders. There's been a big bust up about Precious Grundy. Her father pulled her out of school, and you know how he is, and her Mum found out …"

"That whitefella bin dead by now without us." He spoke slowly.

"Yeah, Dad, probably. Anyway, we need to have a sit down and work something out. Otherwise it's more intervention from above."

"I didn't like the way 'im looked at you."

"I know Dad, I know, but it's just all too heavy right now, okay?"

Her Dad's good eye drifted into the distance and he nodded.

"See ya later doll."

"See ya."

Mirrin walked outside under a near vertical sun, and wished that the heat would relent, even for a single afternoon.

Andrew Hanson

STETSON

I'm not sure there really is such a place
as Doom, Australia but if there is
that's where he's living with his bed-bound wife,

complaining that she tells him not to put
the light on when he goes to the loo at night,
complaining about his children staying out late.

I remember those long long-ago Sunday roasts
when he told me he'd worked in Papua New Guinea
and had been a Rhodes scholar at Oxford.

I remember his tight-gripping hand and steely-blue eyes,
his two-year-old daughter wanting vegemite on toast,
his wife worried about his low sperm count.

Through the periscope of my imagination
he has become an Antipodean celebrity,
mounted on a white horse, wearing

his Stetson straight out of a Zane Grey novel.
A Billy Graham leading an evangelical charge,
living his mission in Doom, spreading the faith,

trying to rub a pigeon of clay into
        a white dove of peace.

Michael Henry

NOCTURNE II: SMALL TOWN: SMALL HOURS

Much the same as anywhere like this –
curtains drawn on household, anarchies
Spliff Court, Speed Terrace, Crack Court,
small-time dealers, a convenience store.
On softer skirts of town, Gin Alley, Valium Vale,
Jesus Drive, where fervent tongues
blurt and babble like bacchantes,
everywhere desires like weirs are clogged
by weeds thick-stemmed as monkey's tails,
risky love affairs are sprung like panthers
tensed to pounce and rip up reputations.
YOU know the score.

(I come to loiter by your window)

Swingers dice to settle who shags who
in humble houses tarted-up as weekend cots
cheek-by-jowl with others waiting for Sir Midas
to exploit them with his touch: damp walls,
poor roofs, kitchens almost bare, scant food,
haunted by rootless men who need a base,
a fag, and, if in luck, and husband out, a fuck.

(once more I come to stand beneath your window)

Fights, jibes, insults: generations living
far too close. And in the lands of sofa world
and TV makeover, soft sleepers bottle up
contempt and rage, hide it under pillows
primed like guns. Same heart, same feelings
as on the other side of town but practices
a little more hygienic. Nightly dreams of
visitations from a hairy beast.
(You within, your curtains tightly drawn).

Robin Ford

AT THE TEMPLE

Votive sweat. Phones flash to prove the visit,
coaches carry hordes from cruises, let them loose.
The Brothers of Perpetual Tat host stall on stall –
hats, flags, naked gods, some rendered decent
by figleaf or castration – it feeds the kids
through years of drought and starving kine. I too
part of the crowd so just as bad – a snob as well.

The better looking local youngsters work as waiters,
bar staff and, if beautiful, perform an 'ethnic' dance.
Some ply darker trades, bread for winter, hope for best.
Guides bawl legends smooth as worn-down coins,
titillate with hints of lurid tales and secret rites,
gloss over blood and cum, the cruelty at the heart of them.

The old town, picturesque and fly-blown, has come
to terms with pallid nakedness, waxed, glazed, fat.
Some still seek the 'ur' of it, hear lyres and flutes.
glimpse Orpheus or Artemis behind the babble –
but oh and oh the most of them forgot.

Robin Ford

THE FLOOD

*"The end of all
flesh is come
before me for
the earth is
filled with
violence ..."
(Genesis 9:9-
14)*

She likes to lie in bed, listening to the rain
while Saltersgill's streets run like rivers,
all the becks bursting their banks and now
she knows how Noah's next-door neighbours felt
when there was no room on the Ark for them –
      a relief, to be honest,
the drop in pressure now the storm's finally broke,
her everyday scream amplified by thunder.
She turns in her bed, stares at the ceiling,
the last night under the lightning-fork crack
in the plaster, so let the flood come, let it
wash away this shit-hole town, all the bitter-
bartered hate on her phone, barbed posts,
      bullets in the comments.
She dares not pick it up though it's as demanding
as a snotty-nosed toddler she couldn't look after,
no, she won't let herself go there, not tonight.
Did Noah's wife wave to her neighbours
drowning in rising waves as the Ark rode
the swell and sailed, dipping and lurching
into sheets of rain? Mrs Cook over the road
would and Sue in the pub, she definitely would –
the daggers they shoot for her arrangements
for all the things she's had to do but really,
      what's the difference?
Shifting under a single sheet that smells
of her last punter, a touch of Hugo Boss,
she's smouldering like a peat fire, all day the flat
has been a banya, still too humid for a quilt,
the rain on the window sounds like cool applause
for a karaoke slot, and it seems to her as if she's lived
for years as a meme on somebody else's newsfeed.
      A grand exit this,
no encore, no smoke machine, no glitterball,
no party balloons, no farewell cards, no disco lights
apart from crackles of lightning that shock the room,
she always wished she'd been a mermaid, singing
her heart out to a lobster deep underneath the water.
She likes to lie in bed, alone, lulled by the rain.
Let the big flood come to sweep us all out to sea.

Bob Beagrie

SOON ENOUGH

I sincerely regret
To inform you
I'm truly sorry to say
The outlook is grim
Prognosis rather bleak
(When will you learn
You are transient?)
A world of everywhere
Plastic and concrete
You've acquired every
Conceivable convenience
For your disposal
Every variety of voyeuristic
Entertainment – congratulations!
Now that you've reached
Your level of comfort
Your adequate perfection
It is in your nature
To screw-it-all-up
Burn-it-to-the-ground
I get it – this isn't
What you desired
To hear cocooned
In magical thinking
Get comfortable
Witness from your recliner:
Your bombs your genocide
(Oh yes every bullet for
Every child for every school
Shooting belongs to you)
Your obscene disregard
For sky earth oceans
Wind fire flood
Will annihilate us
All soon enough

David Sapp

OR DOLPHINS

If man were so careless as to extinguish himself,
it could be animals inheriting the sacred torch
and if they bungled it, for instance,

the serpents failing to transmit wisdom,
the chimps and orangutans trapped in ranks
of their old, oppressive hierarchies ...

then might not insects be considered candidates
– the roaches, flies and organized bees – or yet birds?
Could not those feathered dinosaurs enjoy a second chance?

But blameless as their creaturely strife for space and mates may be,
does it best our human slavery, rape and war?
Oh let us pass on all this zoo, even stranded whales.

And fainter and less brilliant as that flame may be,
it must descend at last to fungus, plants and trees,
the earth and rock they thrive upon – and sea:

Utterly dependable sea, which held it once before
and feeling it all, is not afraid of catastrophe
or starting all over, again, the whole shebang.

Clive Donovan

It's 10.30pm and it's beginning to get dark.

People are milling around in the town square, being given Chinese lanterns to take with them as they process down to the beach where the fireworks will be.

There is excited chatter from children and, halfway to the beach, a couple of families break out into fairly raucous renderings of what is probably a French football song. One senses it is neither a good tune nor *in* tune, but they are tolerated, encouraged in fact, by the good-natured crowd.

When we arrive, we are first funnelled through the dunes and then the crowd fans out on to the beach. Some sit on the sand. Some have brought folding chairs. We settle down on the not entirely comfortable boulders. The singers have disintegrated as a choral unit but there is still much banter and jocular calling out. Someone yells, "Vive les bleus!" and amusement ripples out through the crowd.

The fireworks begin promptly at 11pm.

At first, they produce fairly modest flashes and bursts of colour but soon things are ramped up and the fizzings and whistles and bangs crescendo and recede and crescendo again through a succession of wonderful explosions for twenty minutes or so.

There are some enormous spherical explosions which burst radially from the rising thin red trace of the glowing fuse, and which spawn within them smaller but similarly expanding spheres, each consisting of bright starlets of colour more or less equally spaced apart. They remind me of the spherical colonies of *Volvox,* a colonial green alga, though to appreciate those you need the narrow view of a microscope. In a similar way the spherical colonies of algae burst open to release smaller ones created within; it's how they reproduce.

Another botanical similarity takes shape. Three or four miles away, the coast of another island stretches more or less parallel to the one we are on. It's too dark to see it but regularly spaced pinpricks of bright yellow mark out the seafront streetlights. But, in addition, there are other, ephemeral lights faintly appearing and disappearing above them like differently coloured dandelion clocks, eerily duplicating our own fireworks and almost more wonderful for their silent comings and goings.

The display on our beach erupts and crashes to a close. Smoke and evocative smells drift away on the breeze. People clap. I wonder: whom are we applauding? The people who coordinated and set off the fireworks or the people who made them? Or the revolutionaries who stormed the Bastille all those years ago?

Someone starts to sing the *Marseillaise* and voices rally to the theme. Knowing only one word of it, and its place, I join in with an enthusiastic "citoyens!", delivered with what I believe to be exaggerated Gallic pronunciation for it is, after all, a wonderfully French French word.

As we trudge back under the stars, accompanied by the pounding African beat of three metal drums, I wonder what the nearby wildlife makes of all this.

On the saltmashes, one-legged waders nudge their heads beneath their wings, seeking quiet, wanting sleep. Perhaps they are wondering what we're up to now: another revolution maybe, or war, and whether or not they should be worried.

They should be, but for different reasons. Ones which will become manifest slowly and insidiously, not with a bang.

But almost certainly with a crash.

Rob Peel

ECCE HOMO/ECCE TERRA
(Behold the Man/Behold the Earth)

Ecce Homo.

Ecce Terra.

Am I the one?
who kissed the cheek
who passed the chalice
of red blood,
who profited in silver

I am the one
who burns the lungs
and drinks the blood
of my own earth
priced in dollars

Am I the one?
who flung the spear
that tore the flesh
when blood and water flowed.
And did I gamble for his clothes?

I am the one
who rings the till
who flings the goodies
into trollies
who flaunts fast fashion
sewn in sweatshops
who gambles on the price of
silver

Am I the one?
who lied three times
the timid friend
no hero him
when the cock crowed

I'm such a one
a quiet witness
a timid friend
no hero I.
Now faith is gone
but I have heard the cock crow

Was I in the crowd?
that freed the rebel
when Pilate said
Ecce homo
Behold the man
the wretched, ragged man

I was there in the crowd
that cheered for the markets
who measured our lives
in branded bags
slimy with oil
Ecce terra
behold the earth
the wretched, ragged earth

So here is the question –
who's on the cross?
the wretched earth
or the tortured flesh?
look closely, what does it say?

Homo Sapiens
Wise man
king of the apes

pinned above our heads
on a cross of our own making,
our conscience hanging from a Yew tree.

But listen …
the cock crows,
and has crowed one final time
as the ice crack and the fire come near
we hold the scales and have the weapons
of cold and passionate science

Now's our last moment
to save our children's children
to roll back the stone of ignorance
And To Cry

'Behold the People/Behold the Earth.'

Justin Lloyde

TALKING TO HORSETAIL

People are scathing,
they don't like how you amass
on the riverbank,

they don't know where you come from,
speak openly about banishment,
how to apply poison.

Once, I tried to haul you
out of your realm. I felt
your muscles tense
as though you took umbrage.

Why did you hold back?
Do you hear through your old tubes
what they're saying: death
to the whorls of all living greens.

If we pull through, please stay
on my plot. Teach me
your arrangement of nodes.

Gill Horitz

Equisetum (Horsetail) – prolific as forests 350 million years ago.

John Napier noticed how the spacing between horsetail stem nodes decreases as you get closer to the top, and used it as the basis for inventing logarithms in 1614.

Narrative # 3

The Water Buffalo's gaze
challenges with the power of self-knowledge,
the burden of ridged, crescent horns borne
lightly on stalwart shoulders,
bowing backwards from the force of his character,
jaw raised in defiance of water demons he once controlled
from his post on the riverbank.
Algae green, flecked with imperfections,
he is glossy like the river, cold to caress.

Broad nostrils flare, puzzled by the absence of steaming clouds
billowing across the idling current,
by the lack of musk, his claggy coat now soapy to the touch,
wide splayed hooves no longer deep in the mire,
the fly-flicking tail wrapped neatly around his bulk.
Succulent grass has been replaced by museum glass,
the water, by the stream of ogling visitors
who do not see
the confinement of blood, bone and hulking spirit,

simply a small, but dignified, jade carving.

Ali Pardoe

PAVEMENT

Below the hedge
dense enough
to think itself a wall,
two pieces of shell
cradle a stare,
this gawping shock of eye
rests on a soupy mess
of feathers and blood
while one spiky wing
juts.
Some force threw out the egg,
a Somme
staked in centimetres.

The birdlet blindly tasting flight
for seconds only
as it fell,
maybe instinct overrode the pain
and nerve tracks
momentarily remained intact
for that magic strain
to lift upwards
free,
free from concrete's
catastrophic pain.

That fearful eye
survived the longest:
a glassy bowl
still filled up
with virgin unparted sky.

Julian Cason

GETTING OUT OF THE HOUSE

Breathless
I stagger from room to room, carrying leaden boxes
the house is abuzz with too many queens,
my thoughts swarm, buzz round and round –
what was, what is, what if –
following an argument, scrutinizing responses,
endless correspondence concerning disputes;
but there are no answers
only fruitless drilling on the windowpane.

Outside tall cypress trees hedge us in –
a wall of malicious tongues, false accusations.
The bees are furious; they are flying like bullets
to a nest-box on the trellis that is hissing
with dissatisfactions, resentments, questions.
Some crawl round the entrance hole
scrutinizing the wood; others zoom
to the box and away and
round and round and back again.

I slow my breathing –
the buzz gives way to a cry,
the high-pitched whine of a chainsaw.
And when I open the door, the bees quieten,
form into a ball; branches start to fall,
floating down like giant feathers.
Now I can see the drive, the sun high in the sky.
where beams of light knife scowling cloud.
The stubble field, its cut-stalks glistening, stretches

into the blue distance, become hazy as gauze
bandages unwinding from a healed wound.

Christine Selwyn

DUMB
ANIMALS

A goldfish on its side,
floating in a pungent bowl,
haunts her bedroom.

I imagine being the victim –
gills clogged with algae,
fins colonised by fungus.

I speak in tiny bubbles,
asking for understanding –
a lifesaving remedy.

The lens of her face
contorts fat and thin –
it bloats, then disappears
into a concave shine.

Only her blur torments,
with tapping fingernails.
Only her ghost probes,
then adds cold tap water.

I return to manhood
as she kisses my neck
and strokes my thighs.
We love as counterparts,
finishing in a paroxysm
of rigor mortise faces.

I'm a rictus animal,
feeling slimy scales
lose their dreaming.

I catch at new breath
and re-enter my loss,
as I watch gold die.

Robin Lindsay Wilson

SHIFTSTONE

November is the shiftstone month
sandwiched between festivity and remembrance

we, too shift
from cotton to cosy
from river walks to frosty hikes
from pumpkins to stirring up
last harvest to first frosts
poppy garlands to holly wreaths

some things stay the same:
dried fruit and the scent of oranges
ringing laughter
the stamping of chilly feet
and ghost stories running right through

Lauren K. Nixon

Darkness hissed.

Yutikaa opened her eyes. Silent, black space enveloped her. She heard Ajay snore. His breath stank of alcohol and tobacco. There was the stench of cheap, department store perfume. It hissed again. Whatever IT was. Blinking her eyes, Yutikaa raised herself slightly, leaning on her elbows. Apprehensively, her eyes scanned the blackness before her. There was nothing. Her head ached. Migraines were a frequent occurrence. She needed to get back to sleep. In less than three hours, she had to be up to cook and clean and get the children and husband ready for school and office.

Sighing, Yutikaa pulled the duvet closer to her chin, shut her eyes and fought to sleep.

It was still dark and cold when Yutikaa woke up to start her day. She prepared eggs and toast for the children and tea and ham sandwich for Ajay. After downing her second cup of coffee, she managed to swallow a custard doughnut while loading up the washing machine.

When the family came down at seven, they settled among themselves and chatted as their mother went about the rest of the chores.

"I've got a soccer match this afternoon. I'll be late," announced Amit, the sixteen-year-old.

Nobody bothered to say anything. Ajay was reading the newspaper. Sumeeta was as usual fiddling with her phone. Yutikaa sighed. Nobody looked at each other anymore. Nobody said anything anymore except if something was needed. By eight, everyone was out of the house. Yutikaa dragged her feet upstairs for a quick shower before she had to head to the supermarket. Her in-laws were coming over for the weekend. There was an endless list of groceries and items to purchase.

As she undressed in front of the mirror, she froze. Her reflection gazed back at her. Her skin was dry and pale, her hair thin and uncombed and her breasts drooped exhaustedly with the weight of the world. The body before her was one shapeless mass of blob. Unforgiving lines sketched under her eyes. She cringed at her lips that forgot to smile. The sound of her laughter was a distant, ghostly echo. Yutikaa turned her back to her reflection and downed her second glass of wine before hurriedly stepping into the shower.

Once again, the darkness hissed. Wide-eyed and unable to fall asleep, Yutikaa sat up straight. She noticed the door to her wardrobe was slightly ajar. It seemed the hissing came from inside. Suddenly, a pair of iridescent, yellow-green lights pulsated from within the blackness. Yutikaa gasped. Beside her, Ajay slept deeply. She considered waking him but after a moment's pause, decided against it. Silently, she slipped out of bed, tiptoeing to the wardrobe. The hissing grew louder. Yutikaa opened the wardrobe door fully.

It was empty except for her frumpy clothes and worn-out shoes.

"I won't be home for dinner," Ajay said flatly over breakfast. Yutikaa stiffened. She learnt not to ask why. It did not matter anyway. Ajay never looked at her anymore the way he used to before marriage and children got in the way. Some nights, when she felt the desire to feel the heat of his skin against hers, she sensed his repulsion. It hurt. The children as usual were disinterested in anything that did not include them in the centre of the Great Scheme of Life.

She began to wonder – was her family worth her life?

That night, Yutikaa managed to fall asleep. Ajay was not back so the bed was all hers and the night was free from snores.

During breakfast, Sumeeta posted selfies as she sipped her juice and nibbled on her cheese toast. Amit attacked his bacon while reading his magazine. Yutikaa sat down with her children hoping for a chat. After fifteen quiet minutes, she rose and resumed her chores. When the children left for school, she went to the bar in the lounge and poured herself a glass of Madeira. Its sweet richness soothed her heart. Closing her eyes, she decided to nap on the settee.

The hiss stirred her. Startled, her eyes searched the surrounding space. It hissed again, this time louder, more persistent, almost calling out to her. Intrigued, Yutikaa stumbled her way upstairs. The wardrobe beckoned her. Her limbs felt loose and her mind felt dazed. It must be the wine. She entered the main bedroom. The door to her wardrobe was open. Taking a deep breath, she went towards it. This time, the hiss was softer, silkier as if coaxing her to peep in. She did. Yutikaa screamed.

Gleaming serpentine eyes gazed hypnotically at her, flicking its forked tongue seductively in her direction. Unperturbed, it hissed a lingering hiss. Scrambling in panic, Yutikaa leapt upon her bed. The room fell quiet. She could hear the hammering of her heart against her chest. The snake slithered but not towards her. It seemed to slither inside itself. Enthralled, Yutikaa realised it was shedding skin. The movement was slow, rhythmic and dance-like. Yutika's heartbeat steadied. Her breathing slowed. In time, the snake surrendered its old skin in entirety. A mound of used dull scales sat tiredly around its new, shining body. Yutikaa inhaled sharply. Her eyes had never seen anything more beautiful in her life.

The born-again snake illumined a radiant golden-brown with shimmering silver tipped scales. Bewitched, Yutikaa left the bed, gingerly walking towards the snake. Unafraid.

Kneeling, she met its eyes. She had seen those eyes before. They were hers.

Alarmed, she fell backwards.

The thud woke her up. She was on the floor next to the settee. Her head throbbed. The clock struck four in the afternoon. The children would be back soon from school. She needed to prepare tea. The telephone rang. Yutikaa struggled to raise herself from the floor. Her hand reached out to answer the ringing. It was Ajay telling her that he was going to be late and not to prepare dinner for him. It was one of those traits she loved about him – his politeness and his habit of keeping her informed. A slight giggle echoed on the other end.

"It's her, isn't it?" Yutikaa asked, levelly. The one with the cheap perfume. Ajay remained silent as a grave.

Calmly, Yutikaa placed the receiver down.

Three Years Later Yutikaa stepped into her new flat. It was small and utilitarian in its presentation. It was perfect. She threw open the windows, surrendering the flat to the resplendent golden glow of the autumn sunshine as it warmly enveloped each space of her home. The struggle to arrive was long, arduous and ugly. Tempers had flared. Fists did the talking. Ajay's family revealed the monsters they really were. Her own family turned against her.

"You are nothing but a shame and dishonour to us!" her mother had spat in her face when Yutikaa, bearing only a haversack filled with underwear, a hairbrush, toothbrush and soap appeared at her parent's doorstep with a bloodied face and broken wrists.

"What kind of a mother would abandon her children?" Snarling, her father had pulled her hair and slapped her on her cracked, bleeding face.

A mother who did everything for her ungrateful children.

"What kind of a wife would dare leave her husband? You slut!" barked her youngest brother, charging towards his sister and aiming a punch in her head.

A wife who refused to be a doormat.

She was not even allowed to stay the night. At two in the morning, alone in the chilling wintry storm, a women's shelter had taken her in. People who were not family and friends received her, cared for her and assisted her in filing a police report. The divorce proceedings further aggravated the bad blood between her and everybody else. Yutikaa refused custody of the children. Let them live with their father and the family and community. Besides, she was in no position to offer them the luxury they were used to. Not having them was a strange relief she secretly harboured. When she thought that thought, she waited.

She waited to be lynched.

She waited to be burnt at the stake.

It was best to keep quiet this thought. It was best to not let people know how unencumbered she felt now – liberated from the manacles of motherhood and family and tradition. The migraines and insomnia almost ceased. She was eating healthier and walking outdoors to stay sane and fit. New hobbies suited her present frame of mind, such as creative writing, bird watching and herb gardening. Like a passionate lover, Yutikaa embraced her exile fully.

With old, toxic skins shed, she enjoyed discovering and exploring fresh layers unfolding inside her, allowing her to illuminate from within. Yutikaa loved the new her. She loved the new skin she was in.

Placing her flat keys on the dining table, she walked around her home, inspecting everything appreciatively. She paused in front of the wardrobe in the bedroom, listening. Only the melodic chirp of the birds on the front lawn outside drifted through her ears. Smiling, she opened the door. New, colourful clothes in keeping with her current lifestyle hung proudly on their hangars and new, quality shoes lined in a neat row on the bottom shelf. Yutikaa took a deep breath.

She stared.

She listened.

She waited.

There was no hiss.

There was no snake in the wardrobe.

There was no more need for the snake in the wardrobe.

Jacqueline Zacharias

TIME'S DECEIT

The clock's hands sweep round, an invention
we devised, precise and measured, orchestrated
to the supposed needs of complex lives.

It ticks to the time of completion dates,
journeys to take, appointments and
assignations to keep. Weighted down
with things to do, it book-ends our
working days, makes excuses for us,
is servant to *before* and *after*.

Yet who notes the exact time and date
in the immediate personal *now* of things –
the first cry of a newborn child
last touch of a loved one's hand
a kiss   a laugh   a slap
a rainbow's shining arc?

No-one but the regulators, the recorders.
Those with rules to keep, required proofs
of duties duly done.

Time is a play we script, learn by heart and
regurgitate whilst *now* waits in the wings
certain sure of its power to halt the deceit.
It closes the curtains, clears the set; opens
them again to stand centre-stage, oblivious
to moving hands, needing no applause.

Patricia Leighton

RITE OF PASSAGE

Frail, strappy, prinked with broderie anglaise –
nothing to it, could blow away

in the wind, fine as a spider's web,
spun for catching flies.

Always, since small, we'd camped on their bed
to empty our pillowcases of festive stash.

But now, where to look?
Mum's conspiratorial smile erased childhood.

Out of the corner of my eye,
Dad became a man-sized shape in the sheets.

My brother, 'til then an unthumbed book,
suddenly flapped open.

Wrapped in that gift came power, heartache, ecstasy.
I tried it on, alone in my room, hooked.

Claire Booker

FORGET-ME-NOT

The name of the boy I once was
is protected by my adult name.
He was called Beloved, in Hebrew,
after a friend of my parents.

It fit, snug as a vest, a sing-song
two syllable sound that became
shortened to one, hollered
across gravel and bags of sand
as I grew into the builder's son.

The name of the boy I outgrew
hides under the cover of my
grown-up name. No one

speaks it anymore, yet it has
an echo, splits, comes printed
upon official letters, sometimes
cries out, insists it still exists.

Bob Beagrie

FOREST SCHOOL SUPERMARKET

Hungry children forage in the forest
to supplement our supermarket sweep

for yellow-labels, and our short shelf life
larder's empty as a squirrel's spring drey.

Learning to make pies out of mud and clay
we're taught how far a little can be spread.

Cheap margarine and marmalade on bread.
Braving brambles and picking ripe berries

is fun. Let us skip past the shopping aisle
filled with fresh air miles of exotic tastes.

We can pick carrots, peas, potatoes straight
from our fields. Appreciate our being

highly skilled as any in a fair land.
We grow from torn flour bags left behind.

Tracy Dawson

REDCURRANTS

I remember their taste
sharp but also sweet
melting in my mouth
lips tainted
with a fiery red juice
they tasted of a long, hot summer
and of grass
burnt by the August sun
I remember my little fingers
boldly reaching for them through the fence
and with a cheeky smile
running off before getting caught
invincible
defiant

the old lady sitting in her garden's shade
was looking with a great nostalgia
at the red-headed girl
stealing away the summer's innocence
locked in a handful of ripe redcurrants.

Jagoda Olender

DANDELION
WINE

We picked all afternoon
for Shakespeare and St George,
each sun-charged yellow star.

Years later, one demi-john, dust covered,
found at the back of the cupboard.
Your written hand. Proper ink.

'Wine. Home-made. Dandelion.'
Your labelling. Faded. And a date;
'Heads – collected April twenty-third' –

the year. That date. I think,
'ten years, two weeks,
one day, what *hour* before you died?'

Today so much remains.
I see you – tall, a fraction stooped,
your hair a silver silken ruff.

We picked all afternoon,
long fingers plucking
geometry of pis-en-lit.

French epithet on each supernova,
whooped with childish glee –
one more delight you gave to me.

This year I came too late,
down the lane, through the gate,
already time-lapse had begun.

Catherine wheels of gossamer,
shutter-speed change of each small sun,
yellow star to fairy globe;

a field of roundels. New life,
feather tipped and shimmering.
Each one a silver silken ruff.

Fiona Shillito

51°16'17N 3°1'24W

Today I took you to the beach.
We parked beyond the row of bungalows where
that woman stabbed her husband over bubble and squeak
and followed the footpath that starts in the churchyard
tunnelling through buckthorn to the sea.

As we skirted the big yellow buoy roped to the wreck
where you sat and smoked a roll-up
that last Christmas you came down, I saw you
hesitate, as if this earlier you was also with us and might
stop for a while, roll another, watch our dead dog
running after his ball but the moment passed
and you kept pace with me.

Even I could see you didn't really want to be here
but you've yet to find a way of evading
the stories that spool through my head, where
walking with me on a winter afternoon can still happen
and all our griefs, all our misunderstandings
lie stranded on mud flats.

Deborah Harvey

FOLDING SHEETS

We would face each other down an expanse
of fabric, bridging the gap,
bed sheet, table cloth, rug, it didn't matter
what it was, but the act of folding was all.
Two corners each, held between thumb and forefinger,
ten year old arms stretched as wide
as they could go, as if trying new wings of cloth for size,
to see how far they would take me, before meeting both corners
together in silent prayer, then grasping a new corner,
making the cloth ripple and undulate like small waves
lapping the shore, flapping my arms
to make it billow, ship's sail in our living room.

Sometimes when her face did not wear
the look all mothers have, when time
is short and chores too many,
I would tug sharply on my corners,
she would jerk her arms, step forward lightly
or drop her corners and laugh,
and the folding became a game
only we knew.

Other times the task would hold no joy,
a job to be done, before the next,
as we both stepped forward, met in the middle with outstretched arms,
she taking my corners with her own,
then deftly giving it a shake, tossing it over her arm
and it became a neat bundle, ready for the cupboard.

I faced her this way over the years,
until it stopped.
She forgot how to fold, didn't know which bit to hold,
didn't understand a corner, didn't recognise her daughter
hanging on the other end as though it was a rope
I could pull on to bring her back to me.
Today, I grasp corners and look up, hoping
I might remember her face as she was.

There is no-one tugging the other end.
Limp cloth pools on the floor at my feet.

Lisa Falshaw

SLEEPING PLACE

August nights unbutton my grief,
Eleanor Rigby on the radio,
net-curtained light
a blotched moon-face
above dark roofs.

I pad across the landing,
ask Mum if I can share her bed.

She answers *yes* –
a long-drawn out sigh –
turns onto her side.

I slide under the covers,
doze where Dad's warmth had risen
from mattress to sheet;
where the bed once held a body-shape
made by his sleeping, dreaming, waking.

Sheila Jacob

York

MOWING THE LAWN

Oblivious to the routine
that swirls around her,
she sits in a flimsy nightdress,
snacking from a trolley,
watching daytime telly
give way to the night shift.

She can't garden anymore.

Nurses visit three times a
day to tend to her needs.
Her daughter now sleeps
over in case of an emergency

The borders have been mulched
to keep the weeds down.
A neighbour visits every
3-4 weeks to mow the lawn.

It's a short-term arrangement.

Alwyn Gornall

THAT YEAR

You cut down a vine and sow a meadow:
cornflowers, ox-eye daisies. You hand-stitch a dress.

Come autumn a nurse takes your blood-pressure
again and again as if the numbers are wrong.

You swallow pills and wake as usual in the small hours.
Balance one prospect against another.

A week of frost. Threads of spiders' webs show thick as string.
Scarfed, gloved and booted you stamp outside to fill

five empty feeders hooked like lanterns
over the starched grass

and wait, head cocked to the faint continuous
crackle from hedge and bush of a thaw failing to set in.

Patrick Yarker

ON REACHING A CERTAIN AGE

which is what the French call it,
too *galant* to mention a number or

corned feet thickening ankles
vein-network nature's painted leg-tracery

shape-changing sagging gravity-favouring
hair thinning greying skin wrinkling turkey neck
chin sprouting eyes watery filmy

what did he say? why do the young gabble?

the wrong spectacles
why is the phone in the garden when it's about to rain?

something we had to remember write it down yes but where's a pen?

how did we get here? for there yet beats a heart
not the pacemakered, medicated, operated one
but the essence of who we remember as ourselves
still susceptible to a glance a smile a jest desire's pulse

in our uncaring red and purple
and battered canvas wide-brimmed hat against the sun
spectacles tinting we sally along the street
a wave – regal? – to the car-driver who has stopped to let us cross
(he thinks we're old)
into a new day
blessed
thankful

Janet Hancock

PLAYING ME

To play the role of me, I'd choose *What's-His-Name,*
the film star in that thing, you know, he played
the husband led on for years by his wife.

No, it's not *my* situation. I'm trying to identify
the actor, but I forget his name –
the one who was the husband in that film,

his wife pretended her affair had ended,
and he trusted her. No, not *me,*
the character in the film, the sorry husband

who forgives his wife. In his predicament
I wouldn't be so wet about transparent lies.
That actor can do sorry alright,

he's not sympathetic – pathetic, more like.
In the audience, your skin would crawl.
Mine did. The actor – my spitting image –

capering like a man with unhurt pride,
self-deceived, ignoring tell-tale signs
she made no effort to camouflage.

You must have seen the film: toast
of the town. The actor's name – forget it.
I'm like the husband, pretending memory-loss,

though I'm not exactly pretending. I simply mean,
in the film of my life, that actor could be me.
Next thing, I'll be forgetting my own name.

John Wheway

I've driven half way across the country to my father's today because he's caught pneumonia. I haven't seen him for a while. I've only recently come to realise how like him I am. At social gatherings my partner Sue does all the talking. I'm there in the thick of things, laughing at the right moments, but I don't say much. My father was like that. Being married to someone like my mother gave him a chance to see things close-up without getting involved. He seemed to know when couples were going through bad times long before my mother, too busy talking, did.

I see him through the bay window, the light on, curtains not drawn. He now has a room for each of his interests. The front room is where he reads. He's standing with a book in his hand. Looking closer, I see he's balancing on one foot. Why isn't he resting? Though I have a key I ring the bell. I'm about to ring it again when the door opens.

"Hi dad," I say brightly and hug him. He doesn't respond. When I let him go he walks to the sitting room and I follow, past the old key-hooks – a tacky souvenir from Knossos where he's never been. He lowers himself onto a settee and I onto the other. He's breathing hard.

"This is where I watch films and TV," he says. He waves his hand at the rows of flowerpots. "Sorry about the house plants. Forgot to water them."

The room looks tidy. No clutter. No sign that Christmas is soon.

"How are you?" I ask, "The call from the hospital scared me."

"Bearing up."

"I saw you balancing on one foot in the front room. Part of the therapy?"

"No. Someone told me at a party that it was a test to see how much you're ageing."

"And?"

"Oh, I wasn't testing myself. I was only practising."

"So what happened, dad?"

"Well, I try to exercise every day. That Sunday the snow hadn't melted so I couldn't do my usual digging or cycling."

Those are his official interests. It makes getting presents for him easy at Xmas.

"Then I had an idea for a photograph."

Photography's another interest. Not random click-and-share but carefully planned. His photographs are more excuses for excursions than works of art.

"So I set off across the fields. I think we took you on that path when you were little. I know it well. The snow confused me though, and all the bloody signs said the same thing – Bridleway. By the time I'd backtracked and found the right turning, I'd done my knee in with all the slipping about."

"Why didn't you phone someone? Why didn't you use Googlemaps?"

"I'd left it at home – I didn't want to be mugged in the middle of nowhere. Anyway, I hobbled on. It's not actually very far. The snow was beautiful, untouched. Not like in town."

Tears briefly well up as imagine him alone in a white, featureless landscape, looking all around, trying to work out the way. I've always felt sorry for loners like him, having once been one myself.

"Weren't you cold?" I ask.

"I was wearing my skiing gear. I haven't given it away yet. The country roads were iced up, so I'd been right to walk. The sun was low by the time I arrived. Snow on the thatch created interesting light effects. Thin smoke was rising from the chimney, and there was a glow from the curtains that contrasted with the white-washed walls. You couldn't fake it with Photoshop. In the front garden was a bench-shaped lump of snow. I took a photo through a frosted cobweb and started home. I was tired. I must have fallen. A dog walker found me in a field. You know the rest. I'll be fine once the antibiotics kick in."

"All for the sake of art. Can I see it? The photo?"

He disappears, returning with his camera.

"I'm thinking of getting a jigsaw made from it," he says, showing it to me.

As I suspected, it was mum's house. She and Ken moved there in summer. They were probably snuggling by their open fire when he took the photo.

"Nice," I say.

"Yes. I've done some other good ones too. Have a browse while I make you a tea. Thanks for coming."

He leaves the room again. I start flicking back through the photos, thinking that there might be clues he wants me to find. They're all landscapes and sunsets.

I remember in my twenties wanting to run away. He has nowhere to go. He had been seeing Ken at village events for years, a familiar face. He's just as polite to him as he's always been – resigned, not resentful.

I hear him fill the kettle.

I met Sue late, having wandered first. I'd been as far as I could in many directions, finding my limits. My father's never explored. I've told him he should do so now. There are travel tours for people like him. I've told him he has to get away from the village. He said that the property market's not good at the moment.

When I say I went far, I don't just mean far away. Yes, I was in a narrow alley in Varanasi when a stampeding cow made me lose my nerve. I camped for a night in the Sahara, sleepless with fear, before ending my Africa adventure. But there are other extremities where I turned back. At the front door of a Liverpool squat I decided at the last moment not to knock. Near Genoa where I was helping in a vineyard, I joined an Art commune specialising in Arta Povera. We made things from whatever we could find. Only when I was invited onto the committee did I decide to come back to good old Blighty and get a sensible job. I don't regret those moments. I'm content to sit back and let Sue get on with organising our lives. She's an Arts Administrator dealing with grants for promising artists. I've told her all about the merits of art retreats, of travelling – how people benefit from the experience though maybe not as they expect or hope.

My mother had been worried about me; thought I'd never settle down. Once I did, she left dad. I keep thinking the two things were related. I knew she'd been unhappy for years, only coming alive in the company of others. I don't know how long the affair had been going on for. When I pop into their place on the way home tomorrow I might learn more – telling her she's becoming a granny might loosen her tongue. There'll be mince pies and a Christmas tree, the smell of fresh baking. Of course I blamed her at first, but like the villagers I could see her point of view. They used to feel sorry for Ken. Now they feel sorry for my father. I might be dad's only visitor nowadays, the only one allowed close enough to see that he's broken. Their friends turned out to be her friends. I know from experience how a single man doesn't get invited to couples' parties. Nobody has tried to pair him up with single women. He's not exactly a catch. He could have taken advantage of the connections my mother had made. Instead, he's become even quieter, reverting to how he must have been in his twenties. He doesn't perform at all well when situations are set up for him. When he sees casual affection between old couples it sets him off. Carpenters' songs in supermarkets are dangerous. And old family photos.

My mother's early influence on me faded. I don't think I've ever learnt much from my father. Perhaps as we become more alike, I'll be able to influence him more. I have tried involving him with groups – local photography exhibitions, gardening shows, book launches. He reads many novels, knowing all the plots. He must have known what was going on. I came here with Sue only a few weeks before they separated. I wanted to announce that we were moving in together. We went to the village fete. Sue grew up in London and found it all so quaint. Ken was running the coconut shy. My father won a teddy bear and gave it to Sue. He and Ken chatted about how the event was getting on. Mum could have interrupted them, dragged my father away, but she was busy embarrassing me by telling Sue about my favourite toys.

I haven't heard any noises from the kitchen for a while. I go to check him.

"So what do you think?" he asks, breathing deeply, sitting at the table before two empty dishes.

"You could have died," I say.

"No, I mean the photos. I'm thinking of entering some in a competition. Mint tea?"

"Just the ordinary. Let me do it," I say, reaching for the cupboard where the tea's always been. I put biscuits on the dishes. Waiting for the kettle to

Dream Catcher 48

boil again I look around, noticing more souvenirs of family holidays – a bottle opener from Istanbul, fading fridge magnets from Italy. I prepare the tea and sit opposite him. His chair legs scrape as he begins to rise. He wasn't always so clumsy. "Let's stay here," I say. I look out of the window. "Remember when it was all lawn?" I say, "Remember all those tennis and football matches we played? I like how you've split it into three sections. It feels bigger."

We talk a while about my uncles and aunts, about local shops that have closed down and houses that are being extended. The biscuits are soft but I finish them anyway. I tell him about our new house. I don't say that Sue's expecting – it's too early. He tells me anecdotes that he's already told me on the phone, how he found £180 in a donated book when sorting for a charity shop. I can see he's tired.

"I've got something for you," I say, dashing to my car to collect a book that I place on the table. "I bought it for you in London, from the Garden Museum."

He turns the glossy pages.

"I thought it might give you ideas on how to use all kinds of old things in the garden," I say, "Shabby chic – rusty buckets and all that. Loads of recipes too."

"We don't get rusty buckets donated at the shop," he says.

"I was thinking that if you're going to join the local Open Gardens event you might need a theme. Like, you know, 'Dig for Victory'."

"I'm not *that* old."

"I bet your visitors will be though."

Silence.

"I think I need to kip now dad," I say, "It's been a long drive, and it's not going to be any easier tomorrow."

He nods. "Your room's ready. Guess I should go up too."

I rinse the crockery before putting it in the dishwasher – a habit I've acquired from him that Sue teases me about. He's already heading upstairs. I catch him up and follow, step by step.

"Goodnight son. I hope everything's ok between you and Sue," he says, before closing his door.

I wonder what he means. Has he noticed something? My old room's hardly changed since I left years ago, except now he's collected the family photos from around the house and piled them here. I wonder whether I should take them away with me when I go tomorrow. I wonder whether he's crying right now. I could never hear what was going on behind that heavy door.

Tim Love

EUTECTIC

Welcome to my cupboard of imperfect treasures:

a muttering of wood ash develops
alchemical blush of barium, titanium –
everything brought to light.

Malleable as clay, I unwrap myself
offer you my wares, my stories'
glinting wit of iridescence.

The cracks and dunts are part of this too,
twice-fired by life, and scared by it all,
brittle as biscuit.

Still, despite and because,
I will step into the kiln with you.
Discover where the hottest places are.

Fiona Theokritoff

Ssh! He's coming back!
We all sense him, his ear to the door,
So we talk about shopping and petrol prices, make jokes
With his wife, not about her the way that he does.
Not a case of 'How could you?' but 'Why?'
Her mascara's still dry, but she's bitten her lip,
Which is white and chapped,
And she's wringing her napkin to death.
He walks in unabashed, runs a hand down her spine,
Like he knows he's done wrong, crossed the line in front of
His seated guests.
So *now* he feels guilty.
"More coffee?" He smiles.
Oh, no, come the replies,
Getting late, it's been great ...
"Won't you stay?" says his spouse,
Her eyes wide like a mouse
Which has come face-to-face with a cat.
Love to stay and chat, but the kids and all that.
Next time, dinner at ours.
By the time we've all put on our coats at the door
He's a glass of Scotch in his hand.
"See you Monday," he waves, "and don't be late."
He winks, but the joke's not a joke.
We each hug his wife,
Give a peck to her cheek, with the standard,
Goodnight. And take care.

Howard Benn

THE DESK CLERK

Once when one of my plays was being produced in a small theater in New York, I rented an apartment in an old building in Greenwich Village. The building had a rickety old elevator and a desk clerk in the lobby, like a hotel, where you could leave your key when you went out, and it was put into a slot where your mail was also collected. The desk clerk was a tall, elderly gentleman, who seemed totally in control of his little corner of the world. He gave the impression that he had seen everything, and nothing could ruffle his coat.

One day I came in from rehearsals and asked him for my key and mail. While we were chatting, I was distracted by the muffled sound of people shouting.

"What's that noise?" I said.

"There are some people trapped in the elevator," he said, casually.

He handed me my key and went back to what he had been doing. I stood in silence a moment. There was no one else in the lobby. The only sound was the muffled cries coming from the elevator shaft.

"How long have they been in there?" I asked.

He looked at his watch. "About an hour."

I don't like to tell a man how to do his job, but I felt compelled to speak. "Shouldn't we be doing something?"

"I already called someone," he said.

There didn't seem to be anything else to say, but it was a little unnerving just to stand there listening to their shouts.

"Couldn't we holler up to them? I think they'd feel better if they knew someone knows they're up there."

He stopped what he was doing and looked directly at me for the first time. His face was expressionless. I didn't know if he was offended by the implication that he had not been doing his job correctly, or if he was simply as indifferent to my words as he was to their shouting.

After a moment, he went back to his filing.

I turned and headed for the stairwell. It was a relief when the stairway door closed behind me and I could no longer hear their cries. I suppose I could have called up the elevator shaft on my own initiative. But what could I have said? "We know you're up there! I don't think we care!"

I'm not sure whatever became of them, or how long they were trapped, or what their moods were like when they got out. But I made an interesting discovery about myself. As I stood panting in my doorway after climbing six flights of stairs to my apartment, I realized that in the time it had taken me to ascend, I had morphed into a jaded New Yorker. Because I no longer felt compassion for the people trapped below.

I resented them for hogging the elevator.

Mark Pearce

We were born knowing to look up
and find a face, the face; without it
there would be no milk to nourish us,
no hands to protect us, no heartbeat
pulsing steadily, the rhythm of our being.

Being is not nothingness when there is
a face looking down on us. The golden
face appears in icons, paintings, statues;
sometimes the gender is not clearly one
of mother, more of the great moon shining.

Now when the great moon seems to cease
to shine, when being feels much like nothing,
we see so many searching hopefully, bathed
in the light of screen technology, waiting for
something we are not born knowing.

Maggie Mealy

STUDENT FLAT

There's a bus stop
across the road
where reality happens
on a daily basis

but in here everything
is getting chaotic,
people phone long distances
or hide under blankets.

When the snows arrive
a man fixes his car
the bonnet raised, face
buried in the engine

In a bed some people
on the cusp of sex.
Names are now withdrawn
protecting the innocent.

Meanwhile, someone
is having a panic attack
in the greasy kitchen
to a lute accompaniment.

Down one corridor
Latvians occupy a bedroom
and form a quick choir
to sing their history

John Short

It Wasn't Just the Downstairs Rooms

but the whole house. Pink had been
Denise's favourite colour, I could tell.

Hints were the pink carpet,
close cover from kitchen to master bedroom

and particularly pink was the back yard
with its own Spanish arch and very big padlock.

Even after I moved in, wisps of Denise hung about,
trying to keep things nice — and pink.

Later she took to clogging up the vac
and made dents in the cushions.

She'd breathe on the mirrors
and generally make a fuss.

I lay back on my emerald settee
and drew my viridian drapes against the night.

Jenny Hockey

The Euphemystics

She met him in Alderley
went up to the Edge
o'er the rain-soaked tops
via the humpback bridge

through the outskirts of town
within reach of the wood
by the hole in the wall
near the Giggling Squid

where they feasted their eyes
but left wanting more
of a covert sign
that they both knew the score.

Simon Tindale

PIT STOP

The seaside run to the Welsh coast
once a one stop for coffee in Newbridge on Wye
is now a 3-stop pit stop.

Despite a half-full tank, I'll need a garage,
buy an unwanted sandwich and ask for the stringed key,
or be spying the Satnav for P-signed laybys:
pit lanes for action as fast as Formula 1mechanics.
Unlock belt and door/sprint/hedge gap/zip/ –
and if already occupied by HGV drivers
caught short between Carlisle and Carmarthen
who've improvised a toilet bowl from worn out tyres,
I'll skip to a strategy for Men of Similar Vintage,
(from the Advanced Motoring Test)
of having wide brimmed bottles racked on the front seat,
and fiddle under last week's broadsheet Film Section,
clocking the new Bond Film at 2hrs and 43 minutes.

Not wanting to be that annoying silhouetted dribble of
senior tickets getting up to the Gents,
maybe I'll wait the pause for the DVD,
wonder if Q can modify my Fiat Panda
to detect the handy between places,
or just hand in my Walther PPK back to M
and revoke my License to Spill.

Steve Harrison

is an archetypal balance scale
like the ancient Egyptians used
to weigh a heart against a feather.
It's a brass steampunk version
that I place in the night sky
to glint and clatter against
a backdrop of the milky way;
it does not judge rights to an afterlife,
it is keeping account
of our entangled lives on earth:
deeds that nurture on one pan,
deeds that destroy on the other.

So while things hang in the balance
what I *need* to imagine is that
every deed is really counted
and even the tiniest acts of hearts
as light and peaceful as feathers
will pile up, pile up, and pile up
on their side of the scale to out-weigh
violence, poison and greed:

there shall be a massive counter force,
acts of destruction shall be catapulted away,
all our heavy, dark, desires shall shoot
through the space between stars,
to a soundscape of hiss like fireworks
then spiral into the gravity of black holes
like water down a plug hole;

and our little deeds, feathered as they are,
shall all fall gently back to earth
in a shower of grace, like seeds.

Angela Howarth Martinot

IT'S IN THE TREES ...

Woke 5.30 to a sense of God.
You do not, you do not dare to say
I'm mad – I don't believe in fairytales.
Yet all those Russians poets grasped
the Orthodoxy without a doubt.

I mean God knows where
it comes from. How can you
claim to be a poet and not buy into
this gift horse in the mouth?
Cheaper than a creative writing course.

Such ringing in the spheres.
To come at last fresh
to a morning And God,
of course, is there – else where
does all this other stuff come from?

All the unexpected lines that
just dropped into your head.
You took this all for granted.
It starts early – it's a morning thing,
an ocean in the ear louder

than applause, in that silence
like a loch setting. Of course
it's God – who else would it
be knocking on your door
at that time in the morning?

Take it. Here in your hands.
Feel it in the trees when life's noise
has been stored away. Feel it devour you
before it departs in the night – Thank God,
for that strange voice in the morning.

Belinda Cooke

REVIEWS

Quiet Flows the Hull by **Clint Wastling**
Stairwell Books
ISBN 978-1-913432-65-2 pp 58 £9.00

Regular readers of Dream Catcher will remember that Clint was a much-valued member of the Dream Catcher editorial team – in addition to a number of other contributions to the literary communities of Yorkshire. Around the time of his terminal diagnosis, Stairwell published his final collection of poetry, which follows the fault lines of previous preoccupations with history and prehistory, the interplay of geology on the natural landscape, and relationships between the natural world and humans, and between humans. Perhaps inevitably, writing as he realized he approached the end of his own life, some of these poems are nostalgic: the final poem, 'Ted Harben', maps Clint's early influences:

"an abiding love of
Eliot, Spencer, Auden, Graves"

and "the creed of 70s creativity."

'Punctual' discloses the layers of history through memories transmitted from his grandparents; 'Door, Wharram-le-Street' marvels at the tales told by archaeology, reminding us that

"'living a fragile peace' is a *modus vivendi* of Saxon, Viking and
contemporary humanity."

A teacher in his day job, Clint enjoyed sharing his knowledge – but it's done lightly, not dogmatically.

"John Harrison dreamed in clockwork", he tells us, explaining "the problem of longitude", adding a more metaphysical dimension to his "charting the way for all to stay on course." The science behind bubbles and the delight of sharing them with a four year old grand-daughter is touchingly conveyed in 'Bubbles':

"Spheres are the smallest shape
for the volume of air, while
glycerine slows evaporation.

None of which conveys the joy
my granddaughter has
on sunny days, for bubbles."

There are poems recounting the pleasures of the elements experienced while out walking, and always present is a sense of wonder and curiosity that yokes scientific enquiry with something more mystical. 'Spectre of the

Brocken' gives us both the rational explanation for this rare meteorological phenomenon and the existential questions it provokes:

"Does the sea reflect the sky?
Or sky the sea and does it matter?"

The poet's tendency to wool-gather, instead of focusing, is depicted with humour and honesty in 'Beinn Gharbh', where he admits his (relative) failure in an academic geological exercise and his acknowledgment that

"I knew I was a dreamer."

Elegaic, wistful, funny, sharply observed; here are dreams compacted into poems which act as a bedrock to your own layers of writing and reading the world around you.

Hannah Stone

Viva Bartali! by Damian Walford Davies
Seren
ISBN 9781781727089 £9.99

The Italian Futurists were obsessed with cycling. Thus, Umberto Boccioni's 1913 painting, "Dinamismo di un Ciclista" (Dynamism of a Cyclist), positively hums with the energy, vitality and motion of a racing cyclist at full pelt. Indeed, but for the fact that he was born a year later, the cyclist might easily be Gino Bartali, the subject of this superb collection. Bartali was an Italian racing cyclist – winner of most Italian races and the Tour De France, twice. He was also a committed anti-fascist and a pious Catholic (Pope John XXXIII apparently asked Bartali to teach him to cycle), which, given that his period of dominance in the sport covered the 1930s and 1940s, made his life, not just his cycling, an amazing balancing act.

This extraordinary story – of a poor boy who rose to the top in a brutal and unforgiving sport, was part of the resistance to Mussolini and who used his fame to assist in protecting and helping many Jewish people escape from Fascist Italy (in 2013, Yad Vashem posthumously awarded him the honour Righteous Among the Nations) – would probably be enough to drive this collection along. Though such collections, with an imposed "narrative" organised around the protagonist's life, can sometimes drag a little as all notable episodes seem to require a poem of their own, there is no danger of this here. Davies is selective in what he covers – the rivalry with Fausto Coppi and Bartali's obsessive search for the drugs he thought Coppi used might perhaps have figured more – while communicating fully the extraordinary story and, most importantly, he has a mastery of description, juxtaposition and imagery which makes the poems zip along like the Jumbo Visma team in full pomp – helped by the decision to write all poems in couplets which do seem like a whirring cycle chain propelling the book forward.

Bartali's first bike was a "…cast-off / butcher's bike, sin-black" riding along dusty lanes which "dyed the tyres / white" ('Vista'). But Davies writes poetry that is far from black and white – the poems are full of light and shadow, joy and despair. There is such cleverness, elegance and fluidity of expression here that you begin to imagine the words ringing like bells from a Duomo in Davies' head and being transferred to the page undiminished. The imagery is precise and economic – "suntans drawn in scalpel-lines / on arms and thighs, molasses - / dark" ('Anointing'). Davies seems to be able to enter Bartali's mind and understand his driving forces. There can be few better captures of the isolation and obsession of the racing cyclist than "…you were racing / no-one but the goggled motorcade // and someone's shadow / cubist on the roadside rock" ('Solo').

The book is full of perfect, almost throwaway touches. Bartali, the "L'uomo di ferro" (the man of iron), becomes the "man of frost" after a mountain ride, the "man of ash" after a dusty one – the grit and grubbiness of cycling got across succinctly. Lying in his coffin, his great rival Coppi's "…profile was a tour-stage / map – glazed lips the foothills // peerless nose the final climb." ('Summit'). The marvellous imagery giving an immediacy to the poems.

One of Bartali's favourite phrases roughly translates as "everything's wrong; we'll have to start again" but one feels he would have approved of this collection and be quite happy to stop when reaching the end. As a poet and a cyclist if there was one book I would have rejoiced to have written, this is it. Read it. Viva Bartali! Viva Davies!

Patrick Lodge

Dynamo by Luke Samuel Yates
the poetry business
ISBN 978-1-914914-43-0 pp 62 £10.99

smith|doorstep, aka the poetry business, are to be commended for following up Yates' earlier pamphlet debut (he has also published a pamphlet with Rialto), in bringing out his first full-length collection. It is a deeply satisfying read, accessible but never bland, 'relatable' (if we must) but never self-obsessed. Yates straddles a line between the familiar and the fantastic in a series of poems about the Big Issues of life and the minutiae of quotidian experience, viewed through the lens of the poetic imagination. Luke Kennard, endorsing the book, sees in Yates a successor to the New York School of poetry, and it is easy to see that parallel.

These poems demonstrate the best of poetic craft – never flashy, but always clever, especially in the taut, concise endings – such a hard part of the poem to polish, I find. He knows when to stop. A randomly discovered swarm of bees

"… barely moving
but all pointing in the same direction"

becomes a metaphor for the human tendency to become congested (in traffic and at a more visceral level); how often have we found ourselves

"… Going somewhere
but also not going anywhere." ('Going Somewhere').

Many poems suggest the range of possibilities that a really mindfully engaged approach to life offers, without ever insisting on there being one single choice to make:

"I can come off onto the same round
or keep going round", he tells us in 'The Third Way.'

'Birmingham New Street has ten different exits' riffs on a snatched sight of a warehouse denoting "Goods Inward" on one side, creating a moment when

"Suddenly I feel good inward.
The sun warms my legs
like a bull terrier's
breath."

In these poems, seriousness is sharpened rather than undermined by moments of bathos: in 'Stopping the White Man March', the consummate ending gives us one demonstrator

"…forced back
by the police line, falling
into a stand of fridge magnets."

Yates consistently delivers these moments which yoke or juxtapose the banal and the important: look how the recurring seals in "The Bikers" pull together understatement and social critique. And "Can't" uses just 11 lines to create a reductio ad absurdum on the denouement of a relationship. His turns of phrase are delicious: how much he crams into these lines from 'France':

"Out there, in the centre-villes,
French ladies sit, smoking on stools,
their hosiery crossed and manners plaited,
kissing each word goodbye as it leaves their mouths."

Witty, urbane, conversational, and incisive, you will have to search hard to find a collection as readable and enviable as this.

Hannah Stone

Into the Same Sound Twice by Zakia Carpenter-Hall
Seren
ISBN: 978-1-78172-705-8 pp 33 £6.00

One of the recommendations on the back cover of this slim volume declares,

> "(this) debut is a place where 'the ordinary rules of motion' don't always apply."

I immediately thought of the brilliant, and brilliantly accessible, physicist Carlo Rovelli and sure enough, there he is in the second poem, 'Big Talk', when Carpenter-Hall borrows his "Where is the kiss now?" analogy, for considering scale and memory and space, in a cosmological sense, arriving at the conclusion that:

> "We're living in a universe that doesn't make sense
> when trying to approach it through the senses."

There is science, physics and astronomy in these poems, sitting alongside God, family and quiet moments. In 'Tree Art', her mother does her hair for the first time in years,

> "As if using a miniature rake of a Japanese garden, she attended
> to the grove of my hair – so that it barely registered as touch."

Carpenter-Hall is musing on re-establishing the comfort of proximity, nurturing and growth – all of which require time.

One of the stand-out poems is the opener 'Shakespeare Honours My Grandmother', which juxtaposes, and nimbly leaps between, her watching a play and funeral rites happening "four thousand miles away", where

> "...actors as pallbearers carry the likeness / of a body wrapped
> in white cloth, / held together by twine."

'Dust' opens,

> "I heard – out of nowhere – the resonant moans of a cello... I
> can't think in unknown music, Could I be the instrument?... the
> resonance of those low levels of longing and mourning..."

This is the poem that most completely lives inside of and addresses the titular aim of the pamphlet, going 'Into the Same Sound Twice'. It considers space, the bending of light and sound, it asks us to listen: all of which, takes us back to Rovelli.

The title poem itself is a long scattergun thought pattern occasioned by her mixing the words musician and magician as a child, wondering "which artist makes something appear from nothing", an arresting idea and opportunity, which left the feeling that the promise in this opening was not fully realised.

The centrepiece is the fragmented poem 'The Earth-Eating Fire', a 14-part collection of poems or perhaps verses making up one poem – it is unclear – full of rage at humankind's laissez-faire drift into the climate catastrophe, mixed with 'woodland spirituality', which despite being a righteous cause, crafting good lines and sharp imagery, doesn't completely hang together and laments, "but this fire will not cure the climate".

It is an oddly uneven collection: some poems positively sing with their brilliance, their story, while others struggle to retain their unity. Where Carpenter-Hall achieves harmony, it is easy to see a talent that can be expected to blossom in time.

Nick Allen

Love Poems from a Frangipani Garden by **Ramya Chamalie Jirasinghe**
Mica Press
ISBN 9 781869 848231 pp 37 £8.00

It was a great pleasure to meet Ramya in September when she performed at a number of the events in the fabulous 'Contains Strong Language' spoken word festival, hosted in Leeds for BBC Radio 3 and Radio 4 the last weekend of September. (For those of you who enjoy listening to the radio, you might be interested to know that several episodes of Ian McMillan's 'cabaret poetry show', *The Verb*, were recorded during the festival, which may be found on BBC Sounds.)

Jirasinghe's collection is dedicated to the love of her life – her daughter, and certainly the dynamics of love with a partner seem potentially fraught in this elegant and sensuous book of poetry. Indeed, the opening poem warns the reader to

"…look
Elsewhere for roses and promises of
Love ever after or for a knight on a
White horse."
('An Introduction: Cautioning Those Expecting 'Love' Poems.')

There are moments of desire and delight, when

"… Every day I wake up to
The scent of the one frangipani
You gave." ('One Frangipani').

However, the focus of many of the poems reflect the comment made by Jirasinghe's publisher, Leslie Bell, "the sensuous imagery and courageous protest are at the service of a moral mind." In these pages, there is plenty of love in the guise of compassion and empathy, whether for the victims of tsunami, forever living in a world where

> "time will be marked
> by the word
> after" ('Tsunami Villagers'),

or refugees, who

> "... lost count
> of our days and nights, praying for a name." ('Where we are
> Waiting to Enter Europe')

Perhaps the most reliable flow of love is Jirasinghe's evident passion for the world around her, depicted as deserving of more consistent attention and care than we as humans sometimes deliver.

"It's not food that we hunger for", she tells us enigmatically ('Signpost 1: All Things Great and Small'), but the ability to observe the natural world and how it navigates connection and sustainability better than humans do:

> "I must learn from the birds" ('The Birdbath in the Garden').

It is only when "the earthlings ... held a star to their hearts" that

> "Through their leaving, they lived.
> The earth laughed, when finally, it heard,
> the rhythm of its own heart
> in the footfall of the wanderers." ('When we Return')

There are strong images, powerful messages and memorable ideas in this collection. In one or two places, the fact that English is not her first language causes the odd clunky moment, and she acknowledges that "To Write poetry in English in Sri Lanka is to be marooned on an island." I, for one, am glad to have landed on that island.

Hannah Stone

***Bath of Herbs* by Emily Zobel Marshall**
Peepal Tree Press
ISBN 9781845235574 pp86 £9.99

Like the trickster Anansi who is the subject of her research, Emily Zobel Marshall adroitly shapeshifts to showcase dual threads of her identity; her early years in North Wales (where she was conspicuously the only brown face in the village) and the Caribbean heritage that she cherishes from her maternal lineage. A Reader in Cultural Studies at Leeds Beckett University and Vice Chair of the David Oluwale Memorial Association (among other public roles) Zobel Marshall is also clearly a poet of considerable insight and talent (examples of her work may be found in Dream Catcher 45), and it was a real pleasure to read her first collection, published by Caribbean-focused publishers Peepal Tree Press.

The book falls into four sections, each well-focused on specific themes, though common threads may be found in all of the poems. There is a celebration of maternity in the opening (title) poem which honours the traditional nurturing provided to her own mother Jenny:

"Grandmother, daughter-healer,
I give thanks"

or in the 'epic' experience of birthing her own daughter:

"Pleased to meet you,
my beauty.
I'm your mama;
big wave
surfer."

A deep sense of engagement with the natural world permeates many of the poems, especially in the section entitled 'Fell' – a nicely ambiguous term suggesting the northern/Welsh landscapes with which she is familiar, and in which she runs and swims, and also the sense of precipitation. But these are never 'simply' nature poems; they serve to ground her in love of family, and a deep sense of connection:

"and so goes your stroke with death, Dad,
and you strike on, stubborn as an old blue rowing boar
that won't ground onto shore."
('Boat on Pebbles: for Dad')

On a night where she makes a 'Wild Camp' her confidence in the landscape refutes the patronising unsought advice she is given:

"I shall sleep safely here
halfway between earth and sky,
raised closer to the moon,
away from doubting men and
their questions."

It is other men/boys whose unwelcome attentions and behaviours prompt some of her strongest and most memorable lines: I remember wanting to cheer when I heard her perform 'The Reason I Slapped Barry':

"So when you called me *half caste*
you cast me halfway out of my world,
my homeland, my *mamwlad*,
and that slap was for halving me,
though proving that all of it
was mine in full."

Similarly, and with added humour, 'On Leaving the World of Johns' is a beautifully crafted expression of empowerment.

Tender, without being sentimental; righteously angry without bitterness; deeply rooted and shooting new growth in all directions, this is a compelling debut, and the only way to fully appreciate it is to buy and cherish your own copy.

Hannah Stone

INDEX OF AUTHORS

Other anthologies and collections available from Stairwell Books

For further information please contact rose@stairwellbooks.com

www.stairwellbooks.co.uk
@stairwellbooks